GENIUS IS HELD DOWN:
Envy the Biggest Human Emotion

Karen Kellock Ph.D.

Manual for Superior Men

This is a complete theory based on Einstein physics, Political Psychology, Systems Theory and Archetypal Psychiatry.

FORMULA

All success attraction
All disease obstruction
All recovery elimination

You must fast on all three

OBSTRUCTIONS:

People
Habit
Food

GENIUS IS HELD DOWN

The mental disease of the century is narcissistic sociopathy manifested in having no empathy.   I wanted solitude for no one's more hated than he who speaks the truth.   Our self-image is trashed early, determining all that we attract later to confirm that bad identity.   The smarter one is the more messed up they get when wires are crossed, hearts broken, rejected.   Cross a narcissist and it's their entire goal to hurt you as much as they can so don't get involved man.

WRITE OFF YOUR ENEMIES

It's best to write off your enemies. Even if it means to PAY them off, it's the best gift ever bought.

The narcissist: silences that scream and indifferences that betray an obsession. CS Lewis

The narc keeps you in conversations after you're gone. It's not about love but ego after you moved on.

Do the best you can & let God take care of the rest. From what I've read that's how geniuses progress.

It's all you can do not to slip into the swill of a dull, dumbed down culture but I pray you won't sir.

We aren't enlightened by imagining figures of light but by making the darkness conscious. Jung

YOUR FUTURE HAS NO ROOM FOR SHADOWS

The road ahead has no room for shadows you've outgrown. Don't look back/love your home.

There are no losses if you learn to see them this way: they ALL made you who you are today.

What once worked under grace no longer works under judgment. God's removed His hand, amen.

Those with the worst past can create the best future. The bottom is fertile soil for great leaders.

There are NO losses if they made you who you are today--if they built insuperable boundaries, ok?

They think their houses will be there forever. They'll be for a long time, after they've gone yonder.

WRITE OFF YOUR ENEMIES

It helps to look at people problems as **FORCES** not individuals, then it's easy to forget em all.

People interrupt and bug me constantly. A locked gate is the greatest luxury making me so happy!

Your invaders were there because you wanted approval. You must face this, put the onus on you gal.

YOUR SINS ATTRACT DEMONS

Your sins attracted demons. So stop blaming people for it was **YOU** from your lack of repentance hon'.

The alcoholic is hated for what he did while drunk. It wasn't his fault, it's the disease that corrupts.

I'm a true fruitarian, I cannot digest veggies. Steamed cauliflower—tho mushy--sits there & tortures me.

The more you crave to be liked the more you lose yourself. Wanting acceptance is nonsense.

People are not driven by **TRUTH** but by appearances. Not by virtue but by fear and punishments.

The herd doesn't want you to be free, but to be obedient. To smile and blend in each minute.

The more sociable you are the more you dilute intelligence to match the room, to your doom.

People wanna be fake and accepted, not honest and naked. That puts you in exhale, hated.

The mind that dares to rule itself is the true leader of men but the price to pay is hard and tough.

Every single social interaction has a price. Smiling even when uneasy: it's unhealthy to be "nice".

WRITE OFF YOUR ENEMIES

For every micro-second of social discomfort you lose a little more lucidity and clarity--and rarity.

When in politics and life the appearance of virtue is more useful than virtue itself, it is hell.

LIVING SOLELY FOR APPEARANCE

When you're living solely for appearance, you forget how to live with depth, the truly nutritious.

Bad ride: What looks like popularity from the outside feels like mental decay on the inside.

People aren't smiling at you but your mask. You start to believe the mask is who you are, all blanks.

The group doesn't want wisdom, it wants comfort. Be smart, don't outsource your wisdom to it.

When the fire in your gut is replaced by politeness and your replies become scripted, you've had it.

Stupidity has one master trick: it makes you feel smart as you conform but inside you're just a hick.

The whisper "everyone likes you" drowns out the roar of your real self while smothering it too.

The price for being liked is losing you edge. You used to have real panache and that was your hedge.

When you want to be validated so badly you'll betray yourself for a heart emoji and it's tragic see.

You're not filled with anxiety, you're just overdosed on sociability and that's why you need therapy.

It's not about being a hermit but thinking without interference. For that you must cut the audience.

WRITE OFF YOUR ENEMIES

Stop seeking applause. Machiavelli never begged to be understood like the bully in the neighborhood.

IF YOUR READERS AREN'T READY

If the "reader isn't ready" you shouldn't care. That's the spirit that's missing, that makes you so rare.

True intelligence doesn't beg to be received, it just IS and for that they're begging on their knees.

True intelligence radiates, polarizes and divides. It simply exists and cuts them down to size.

The group is allergic to self-respecting minds that can't be molded. It hates those who can't be scolded.

You're "arrogant, difficult, cold, detached" if you can't be controlled and thrashed, called "trash".

You remind them of the freedom they gave up and that makes the uncomfortable so they rise up.

Your clarity becomes their curse. Will you be soothing their discomfort or in truth making things worse?

THE GOLD FAST

Written and illustrated by Karen Kellock Ph.D.

Fasting is part of our program. It's like stepping into an adventure for the weekend, plus getting slim.

Fasting is getting ready for a launch: of something new, big and brave. Now do it, and be staunch.

Fasting is a way of making gold. Food can be a substance abuse and fasting fixes that too.

It's only 72 hours from Friday to Monday breakfast but it will make gold and start new life, I promise.

Fasting is THE way to get inspiration for that new launch. It's a breakthrough after a hunch.

THE GOLD FAST

The scales have a way of crawling up but it's not just about that. We wanna be in control, got it?

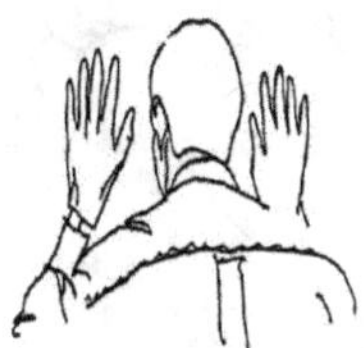

We all tend to use food as a coping device, a go-to to avoid anxiety or make us feel happy/nice.

Food-as-device becomes inveterate and that's the dross we wanna burn away in this minute.

You were born unique but took on a false self. The fast will take you back to the great design itself.

If you HAVE to eat, may I suggest a safety net: a tab of almond butter/few raisins—mouse meals like that.

Spend more time outside, like a child on Saturdays. This is where your insights lie: in wild play.

THE GOLD FAST

It's so nice to know this is the last step in the Hero's Path, the opening to a great life so vast!

The fatigue, hopelessness and dullness of the herd will now be gone and you'll have real ZIP hon'!

We eat and use food to deal with anxiety see. It dates back to birth so the fast makes us free.

I see the weekender as a wonderful vacation with so much promise. Do it and you say "I got this".

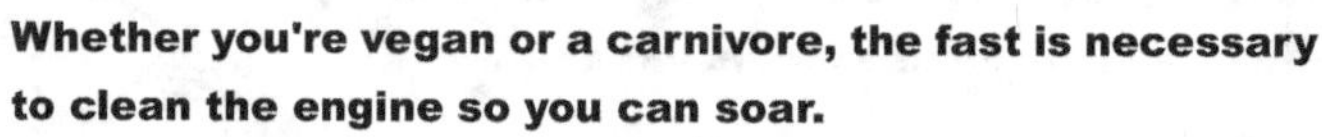

Whether you're vegan or a carnivore, the fast is necessary to clean the engine so you can soar.

See this fast as a weekend adventure of self- and God discovery and you'll LOVE it for sure.

THE GOLD FAST

Anyone can eat, keep telling yourself that. This is something extraordinary and so vast!

We MUST take a break from weight gain and ill fame. This will separate you from the herd [insane].

To get to something we've never had we must do something different, and the fast is that.

Pride in self is necessary to release gold inside to get to heaven see. The curse is reversed, happily.

The weekender is like taking a trip. A proprioceptive journey bringing self-satisfaction and zip.

They brag, they eat. They brag, they eat. What's the pride in that? it's the herd which you will flee.

THE GOLD FAST

Don't tell anyone, this isn't something to brag on. They'll try to talk you out of it so fast in silence hon'.

Take a picture of your bloated self on Friday and by the end of the weekend take it again, hurray!

Medications have thrown everything out of whack. Fast to rid bloat, being lopsided and all of that.

One can be so bloated he's lost all his unique lines. These you want back, they are so FINE!

The fast will separate you from the herd: the quickest way to transcend the ordinary I've heard.

THE GOLD FAST

It's only a weekend but it makes a world of difference. It will be miraculous change so give it a chance.

The scales were crawling up from heartburn pills. This ALL will be gone soon by buttressing your will.

Whenever one brags about their doings, think: yah but have you fasted? No, they can't stop eating.

Fasting is a quick way of becoming a knight. Overcoming SELF is the great dividing line.

The fast gives you FOUND TIME. A million more minutes you usually waste on that common pastime.

THE GOLD FAST

Do you have enemies? Just watch them eat. Transcend your world full of boasters, thieves and cheats.

Your art will find perfection now. This was the last phase of your development for the show.

Have people encroached? The fast will build a wall and separate you from those below the most.

You'll think thoughts you never thought, you'll get hunches for future launches [a lot].

So get excited for your weekend trip. Like a Saturday in childhood full of adventure and hope/zip

THE GOLD FAST

Fasting is the way to get ahead fast, to quickly jump to the front of the line when out of gas.

I'm a holy roller for fasting, a way for winning & a lost art mentioned in the bible as much as praying.

Congratulations! Because you read this far you're on your way to a whole new life and I'm sure you'll be gold-fasting a lot, maintaining a slim physique and slowing/reversing the aging process [almost completely.]

MODERN FRUITARIANISM:

How to Make Gold

KAREN KELLOCK Ph.D., Fruitarian

A new theory in psychology based on Einstein physics with a general formula for all life sciences: You're about to embark on an inner journey of excitement and power. This is a SCIENTIFIC DISCOVERY with a general formula:

ALL SUCCESS IS ATTRACTION
ALL DISEASE IS OBSTRUCTION
ALL RECOVERY IS ELIMINATION

The three obstructions are

PEOPLE
HABIT
FOOD

MODERN FRUITARIANISM

Dissolve your obstruction and you'll snap to your goals, waiting in the wings.

INTRODUCTION TO FRUITARIANISM

Release your obstruction and you SNAP to your goals, waiting in the wings. This will be the happiest day of your life. The great saints said upon this full repentance "Oh, why did I wait so long?"

This book is mainly on the third obstruction: FOOD [and other substances]. I believe food accounts for most mental disease, as there is a direct relation between gut health and mood. There is no worse feeling than being constipated or on the wrong diet.

FOOD [OBSTRUCTION #3]

Man is a fruitarian, like all apes. He is omnivorous, meaning he *can* adapt to other diets like KETO, but glucose [sugar] is the first choice of the human body for energy. This is sweet fruits, greens, nuts and seeds. These are all found in nature and bring man his highest energy and joy.

STARCHY FRUITS. Corn, beans, rice and wheat are also fruits botanically, as they are born from the flower of the plant. In this list I would include popcorn, our healthy snack. They are not fruits in the culinary sense [how we usually see fruits] but in this theory, we only care about the <u>botanical definition.</u>

ONE MEAL A DAY [OMAD] AND SMOOTHIES

These starchy fruits are our breakfast and they are so satisfying one meal is sufficient. You will now be slim, slender, fit and skinny! I

MODERN FRUITARIANISM

believe there is no other way. Start your day with orange juice, your smoothie, then your starch meal in a three hour window. That's it for solid food until the next day, but you can have fruit smoothies or juices.

You'll be flying high now. **ENERGY OFF THE CHARTS**, both from the fruits but also the energy release from fasting. This is because 85% of our available energy goes into digestion. It starts with digestion, then assimilation, then elimination--85% ! This is now released to **MENTAL ENERGY: BEING HIGH ALL DAY.**

This is a low fat diet, as it is true the fat you eat is the fat you'll wear. However, if you get ravenously hungry later take a teaspoon of almond butter, that suffices for a meal and you'll be satisfied. The hunger will be gone. Another "safety net" when you slip is raisins. They make a great quick meal and they are very detoxifying and mucus-binding.

MUCUS: THEORY OF ARNOLD EHRET

Today I had just an organic banana, raisins and dates for breakfast. This I would call a camouflaged fast, since all-sweet fruit is **MUCUS BINDING**. This theory originates from Arnold Ehret, the father of fruitarianism. He showed how foods are either **MUCUS CREATING** or **MUCUS BINDING**. The former is **ACID** , creating mucus and the later is **ALKALINE,** *eliminating* mucus. He saw mucus as the basis of all disease, drying like an eggshell ad filling the cells with ugly and dirty matter. The result is. human ugliness, aging and obesity!

When we fast or just eat juicy fruit, the mucus is broken down and goes out. That is the dissolution of the **FALSE BODY** which is layers of ugly matter distorting our true body, or the "causal body". The fruitarian begins to look like "himself" again, not the cultural distortion which is plump, husky and pasty. His skin becomes ruddy and clear, like a saint. No matter what his age, he **DE-AGES** and this is human beauty. The false body ages quickly--prematurely--and thus old age is a painful decline in hospitals.

MODERN FRUITARIANISM

All disease has the same basis--mucus and acidity--so it's just the **LOCALITY** of the obstruction of mucus that determines the **NAME** of the disease. It's all the same, the universality of mucus, and thus *all one disease* despite the many medical labels.

One should be light, slim and ageless all through life. He should do his best work in his nineties, like Picasso and Frank Lloyd Wright, and progress steadily until one day all systems stop and he dies. **PROGRESS** until the end, not regress, decline or deteriorate. He should be beautiful in his old age, a peculiar and striking beauty from years of wisdom. Not a sorry picture of old age that makes us all shrivel in fear of it. It should be **GLORIOUS** not **HIDEOUS**.

BEAUTIFUL AGING

You should have a spring in your step until the end. With all obstruction gone---from mucus-binding fruits and daily fasting--your body will stay clean and energetic until the end. Just imagine all the foods people eat, with no consciousness whatsoever of what it is they're eating--and you can see why they decline in hospitals in the last decades of life. After 60 the problems begin, and they are nasty and painful.

The state of the human body is filthy. The average person has 25 pounds of retained feces! Some autopsies show 100 pounds in the case of the morbidly obese. The fact that they last even 50 years on this earth is itself an amazing miracle. Now just imagine a clean body, daily eliminating, and you'll see a **MORE** energetic specimen as the years pass. For he has learned what works best for him [we're all unique] and thus has become more efficient. He can enjoy his everyday life until the end.

This is the most important day of your life because you picked up this book. Now you can **SEPARATE** from the sorry human race who is trudging along totally dependent on the medical profession steeped in over-prescription of drugs making **BIG PHARMA** the richest organization on earth. The meds depend on us being **LIFE LONG PATIENTS** on these dangerous drugs, particularly the **PSYCH DRUGS** [SSRI's] like antidepressants, antipsychotics and benzos. But it's no surprise people are depressed with so many pounds of fecal matter inside, or entrenched in sick relationships or lifelong bad habits making them old way before their time.

These drugs are killers, make the depression and anxiety worse, and are hell to get off of. Sometimes the tapering process alone must last years to prevent a tragedy. Every 11 minutes there is a suicide from these drugs. Don't start--go on **MODERN FRUITARIANISM** and be happy for life.

AGES: ADVANCED GLYCATION END PRODUCTS

The medical profession and many health leaders are **DOWN ON SUGAR.** But the thing that ages us is **AGES: ADVANCED GLYCATION END PRODUCTS,** and these are caused by **FATS.** Sugar has a **ZERO** rating! Sugar doesn't age us, it's **FATS.**

NATURAL SWEETENERS

We can have natural sweeteners on my program, like maple syrup. Yum! Have that on your bread. I do not have a fear of sugar like many health leaders so have all the sugar and carbs you want! Sugar makes us happy, energetic and it releases serotonin [the purported reason for the psych meds]. Always recall that children have a **SWEET TOOTH** before their tastes are perverted [ii.e "acquired tastes"]. That is how it should be, for the first choice of the organism for energy is **GLUCOSE** and all starch turns to that.

THE IMPORTANCE OF BREAKFAST

Traditional fruitarianism propounds a light breakfast [fruit only] or fasting until noon or afternoon. I say NO. We must be like the old times, when people had to fuel the tank early before working in the fields all day. I get hungry and I need a **HIGH-STARCH** breakfast to satiate all day. Now fast until tomorrow and you'll be **POWERFUL.** I eat the Ramadan way: break-fast before dawn. By the time the world arises, I've eaten, digested and cleaned the kitchen. Now no more eating. You'll be amazed at the **FOUND TIME** in your day now, since 85%

MODERN FRUITARIANISM

of our energy is taken up in eating, and 85% of our precious time. This is the only fast that begins with a feast! There is now no reason to not look forward to your daily fast.

FASTARIAN AFTERNOONS

I love having my food time "behind me"--where now there are **NO** thoughts of food or desire for lunch or dinner. It's all mental energy now. The energy is up in the head not down in the gut digesting, like everyone else. That means **TOP SPEED AND CREATIVITY.** I love **KNOWING** I'm fasting for the day--that's half the fun of it, what I call **FASTING CONSCIOUSNESS.** It's cornucopia, fantastical, paradisiacal. It is **FANTASTIC.** Everyone else is down in the gut digesting but you are **UP IN THE HEAD CREATING:** *SUPERIOR.* Modern fruitarians are not only clean food wise, but in their homes, head and personal relationships. Now that you have the diet as we do it, the rest of this book is on releasing obstruction from your head and home, for what good is the superior diet if your homelife and life in general is a wreck?

FUN LIKE A SATURDAY [LEISURE]

Crucial to this theory is the importance of **LEISURE.** Stress is a major killer, a reason for our speedy degeneration! **AGING** happens prematurely in our modern age, due to stress. The stress of families not staying together, marriages falling apart, career disappointments and treachery in transitory relationships. We don't stick together anymore. To compensate **LEISURE** has never been so important. **GENIUS** has a capacity for leisure, which propels his work and brings inspiration. **WOULD-BE GENIUS** has an incapacity for leisure, and he remains a loser.

Leisure is important for **INSPIRATION.** Inspiration only "comes up" from the subconscious when we're in a relaxed state, not a workaholic one. **STRESS** kills inspiration. We need inspiration to **PROSPER,** so we can afford a home and transportation. **Homelessness** is everywhere. Home is important for protection from the elements and other people--**PRIVACY AND SOLITUDE** is part of the leisure we need for

MODERN FRUITARIANISM

inspiration, to succeed. HOME IS ALL, WHERE WE WALK TALL. Hippies put down money--how stupid. If you don't respect money, you'll be mooching off of other people. Clear out obstruction, eat right and have leisure for inspiration, so you can prosper and enjoy your lovely homelife.

THE PAST: BAD MEMORIES

Obsession with the past is a horrible prison. Bad memories--retained grudges or unforgiveness--propels ADDICTIONS of all kinds. Anything to escape the stress from bad memories. We must forgive people [in order to detach/get free of them] and ourselves. Jesus died on the cross so the past could be ERASED and that is our greatest blessing. Go for it!

In the past, steeped in obstructions [sick relationships, bad habits and dysfunctional food] we weren't ourselves. We were the FALSE SELF, a compensatory and fake persona for the sake of appearance and acceptance. This is *not who we are*. Karl Jung stressed the importance of finding the TRUE SELF. It is entirely peculiar and unique. Insofar as we find this true self we come to God [who designed it before our birth] and insofar as we find God we come to this True Self. It is the basis of joy and success, nothing else. For God planned our prosperity--He wants us to prosper. {Everyone needs money honey}.

PEOPLE PROBLEMS {OBSTRUCTION #1]

People can be a terrible prison too. They can obstruct even more than food. Bad food habits wreck the digestive, which kills the mood. But people problems wreck the mental, which obstructs the digestive. Controllers [e.g. narcissists] will keep you in a psychotic bubble long term and this is most destructive to body and mind.
Sick relationships will make you old before your time but happy healthy ones will make you an ageless, creative child.

BAD HABITS [OBSTRUCTION #2]

Sin, or bad habits, is ENERGY RECYCLED IN OUTWORN CHANNELS. They put us out of grace. Sin contains it's OWN

MODERN FRUITARIANISM

punishment. For every time we relapse into an old sin, there is a compensation in the present moment and that is how "people can tell" as our aura becomes dull and grey. Sin is hooked to bad memories, which now come up. Sin blocks energy and even constipation can set in. This is all BLOCKED ENERGY. The thing with addiction is its self-reinforcing so we NEED IT MORE BUT ENJOY IT LESS. This is an automatic process, since every time we "give in" to a desire it becomes more reinforced. The bad habit maintains itself and becomes more stubborn to change.

ENTER EINSTEIN: IT'S ALL JUST ENERGY

Einstein proved that everything is just ENERGY at different rates of speed. The fastest energy is MIND ENERGY but this is blocked with obstruction. Einstein also proved there IS NO PAST--the past and the future are right here, now. When we sin we start thinking of the past but when repentant the past is erased and we can go onto the future. We wanna stay QUICK, ALIVE, VITAL, VIBRANT AND JUBILANT.

Bogged down with the past, life is sludgy and pure drudgery. Clear, we enjoy our work even the most menial. I enjoy being a homemaker for my husband as I order our home. For a clean unobstructed body is PERFECT ORDER as God ordained. I'm no feminist. I enjoy my role of homemaker because that gives me control over what I see as the MOST important thing: THE HOME.

HOME IS ALL: WHERE WE WALK TALL

For man is an adaptive animal: he ADAPTS TO HIS ENVIRONMENT. If his environment is orderly and clean he will be inspired with *creative action*. Heaven is clean order and hell is DIRTY DISORDER. That inspires no one and the mal-adaptation is addiction and other stress-relievers. Men are bigger and should take care of the outside duties and cars, women take care of the inner duties like cooking and ordering socks. This is an OBVIOUS DIVISION OF LABOR. The old ways are best.

MY TWEAK ON FRUITARIANISM

Fruitarianism has been called the Superior Diet and indeed it is. When I tried it at first I went miserably wrong. I had read Arnold Ehret *[Mucusless Diet Healing System]* and instantly saw the logic of it, but failed totally when I approached it all wrong. I went out and bought truckloads of juicy fruit and felt bloated, sugar-inundated and UNSATISFIED, dreaming of pot roast and gravy at night. When that gap can't be bridged one ends up obsessed with food. In fact it developed into an eating disorder for years: knowing on the one hand how superior the diet was, but possessed with cravings of culture food, which I feared but had a magic pull on me. Obsession is a terrible thing, a haunting companion. Now I have a different approach and I'm high as a kite and SATISFIED all day and night. I never fall off the wagon because I know myself and allow a safety net when I start craving other things. I know what to eat then, to stay on the fruitarian gravy train.

My present routine is a mango or strawberry smoothie in the morning containing organic greens and a little almond butter for body. This makes me extremely elated and satisfied all morning. Later I have my "starch fruits" which are rice, beans, corn or wheat. These are botanically fruits as they are birthed in the flower. Fruitarians eat fruits, greens, nuts and seeds and that's it. I am so much happier doing my own thing rather than following diet gurus on the internet telling me how to do it. I remember drinking ten-banana smoothies following these types and ending up gaining weight and feeling miserable. You simply must find your own niche.

General fruitarian caveats: no animal, dairy, processed or inorganic foods.

MODERN FRUITARIANISM

OMAD: One Meal a Day

I do best on one main meal a day and so will you. I choose to "get it over with" in the morning so then I can fly in fasting consciousness the rest of the day. The FAST is the thing, not the eating. Eating is a transitory pleasure—it's here, then it's done. Eat within a 4 hour food window then fast 20 hours a day. If hungry the rest of the day, stick to fruit juices or smoothies.

FAT-FASTING

This brings us to FAT-FASTING, my alternative way of living. Holding to low carb, we eat SNACKS [not meals] of FAT: e.g. a tablespoon of almond butter. As is explained in *Champion Guides**, fat evokes GLUCAGON, the opposite hormone to insulin [evoked by carbs]. Glucagon puts us in BIOLOGIC UTOPIA, doing such nifty things like putting us in fat-burning mode [living on our own fat], and eliminating all water retention and inflammation thus releasing incredible energy. We are never hungry and instead of heavy meals stealing our energy we go from snack to snack, keeping the belly flat

REVERSAL DIETING
From Low Carb to High Carb Fruits/Leaves, Nuts/Seeds

I mainly stick to HIGH CARB/LOW FAT. I get a hankering for oranges, indicating a need for vitamin C, and splurge for days. In September my neighbor has her annual green grape harvest and I take the Grapecure for two weeks: just grapes. Reversal dieting is closest to historical nature: when there's a harvest, that's the predominant pick and what we should be eating: that's fruitarian-paleo living. Then some may reverse from the sugar inundation back into lowcarb ketotic "biologic utopia" [glucagon-based}] dieting. Don't let anyone pigeonhole you into

MODERN FRUITARIANISM

one particular diet, reversal dieting is the most natural. Man eats a blueberry harvest and then he fasts until he comes upon another of nature's abundances. Reversal dieting, fasting and full-on fruitarianism will give you an ageless life where your appearance matches your spirit's unique design as in your youth. People depart from this through years of wrong eating which puts layers of encrustation [ugliness] on called "aging". The good news: it doesn't have to be if one restricts to GOD'S FOOD of fruit and leaves, nuts and seeds. Then he will quickly detox all the "layers" of the false body—the non-you—which is such a disappointment to those who fear aging. Plastic surgery is not the answer, fruitarianism is.

EHRETISM [FRUITARIANISM]

The fruitarian theory is based on Ehretism, by Arnold Ehret [1854 German scientist]. He found all disease and aging coming down to ACID in the body. All foods other than produce causes MUCUS [acid] which goes throughout every cell and encrusts [uglifies] the body. When young people resemble their unique spirit but with the years of wrong eating, a false body develops in layers and this creates UGINESS, also known as signs of aging. All foods other than fruit/veg create acid in different degrees, meat being the worst—and all fruit/veg BINDS, dissolves, and takes the mucus acid out. The result is BEAUTIFICATION and DE-AGING. What is aging? Simply layers of mucus, dried like an eggshell and encrusting every cell! When I read Ehret in my twenties I immediately saw the obvious logic to it and have seen the world that way ever since.   Ehretism is basically fruitarianism, which is HIGH CARB.

VARIOUS REVERSALS

MODERN FRUITARIANISM

High carb, or living off sugar, is the engine's first choice of energy. Fat-adaptation, or low carb, is a necessity at times for survival. Man is meant to come upon a berry harvest and splurge, then fast for awhile, then come upon a beast feast and live off that for awhile. That's the paleo man, man's first dietary adaptation. I get sick of dieting sometimes and eat what I want, high or low carb. As long as it's one meal a day, no problem, and all goes well. The blender is a wonderful modern adaptation, as we can put various fixes in it. The varieties are endless and delicious, with no excuse to stay sick anymore. Occasionally some of you may want to REVERSE DIET to meat or a cheese omelet for breakfast—have at it! Now you know how to [reverse] do it. Have at it! Just have that be your one meal and you'll be fine. I'm not judging anyone, I personally just don't do well with fauna [animal flesh] and I eee how much better I feel when returning to fruit-only [which includes corn/wheat/rice/beans].

TACOS [HOMEY FOOD]

I grew up in Southern California, living on TACOS almost exclusively. It's comfort food because emotionally it takes me back, much like spaghetti or pizza would for an Italian. This influences the BODY: happy thoughts. I use corn tortillas, cheese, lettuce, black olives and salsa. Sometimes I get so sick of dieting--someone else's notions--I switch back to homey comfort food: TACOS. The fresh salsa, lettuce, olives and corn tortillas are FRUITARIAN. And the cheese makes it LACTO-FRUITARIAN. Cheese has as much protein as meat and is important for an older person. At these times I say to hell with dieting and diet theories altogether! Recently I grew sick of the sweet and starch, and hankering for home: TACOS! I don't even regard this as a "cheat day" but a HEALING day. For in paleo theory, our _first food-adaptation_ is the healthiest, whatever it was. Was it bread, pancakes, omelets, tacos? Go for it and dream of happier days.

LIBERATING FOOD CHOICES

This gave me a sense of liberation in food choices, recognizing that someone else's diet theories didn't work for me—even if they do have a perfect physique. It's incredibly freeing to strip away from the pressure to conform to someone else's dietary choices--to find your own way, to achieve your own health goals. The key is the realization that everyone's body is different, and the point is how we FEEL not that ideal physique of someone else. Eating foods you love like tacos makes life enjoyable and sustainable and contributes to overall well being. Will you now acknowledge this separation as major PROGRESS, a significant step towards a healthy relationship with food? Celebrate the journey!

This newfound perspective was empowering, as psychologically it made me think of happy sunny home life in La Mesa, my hometown, with the freshness of the lettuce, olives and salsa. And the protein in cheese was such a boost for the day. Connection to roots is a real thing: Comfort food that reminds one of home evokes positive emotions and contributes to a sense of well-being. This emotional connection enhances life and meals. In my case tacos with their vibrant flavors and fresh ingredients transported me to joyful moments in the past which was a rocket launcher on my mood and mental health. Nostalgia is healthy. Consider the protein for muscle mass and salsa, olives and lettuce for vitamins, minerals and fiber. Having a protein-rich breakfast made me feel full and energized with a positive tone for the day.

A CLEAN SLATE

One of the greatest outcomes is what fruitarianism does to the mind and emotions. I had so many resentments, a severe case of PTSD I couldn't rid myself of. The memories would come back all the time without warning and I'd be angry again. I'm ashamed to say! But I

MODERN FRUITARIANISM

honestly could not wipe these tendencies out, even seeking various therapies to do it. UNTIL I adapted to fruitarianism and my whole universe changed. The slate was cleansed: I had only happy memories of the past and all was forgiven. It wasn't a matter of forcing forgiveness, it all just happened naturally like fog being cleaned from a mirror. I had no more bad feelings for anyone as the body was cleansed and my brain and heart purified. I had the attitude of a baby: happy and bright, fascinated with life.

*There are five books by Karen Kellock on fat-fasting: *Champion Guides, Arts of Paleo-Fasting, Daily Fastarian, Ageless Cornucopia and Just Skip Dinner.*

GENIUS IS HELD DOWN:
Envy the Biggest Human Emotion

OUR SELF IMAGE IS TRASHED EARLY
ATTRACTING CONFIRMERS OF TRASHED IDENTITY
MUST BE EXCLUSIVE AND SELECTIVE
FEMALE GENIUS IS RARE SIS
RETICULAR ACTIVATING SYSTEM
THE MISWIRED BRAIN IS ABOUT SURVIVAL
MISJUDGMENTS LOCKED IN MUSCLES
TO YOUR *NEW* NEURAL PATHWAYS
WE GROW BY OVERCOMING BAD FRIENDS
SHOCKED BY FLIP-FLOPS
FORGET DETAILS: THROW THE BAG OUT
LOSING THE HEDGE OF PROECTION
SEEKING APPROVAL OF RASCALS
IT FEELS LIKE ETERNAL GUILT
RECAP/THOUGHTS ON THE GREAT WORK
THE PAST AS A DOC ON YOU
SISTER ABUSE
UNREALIZED JEALOUSY
ATTEMPTING TO BE SOCIAL? WHY
EVERY DAY SELF-CHOSEN
LIBERAL LIARS AND CHEATS
IF YOU WANT IT YOU AIN'T GETTING IT
SICKLY CYCLICITY
OBVIOUS DISRESPECT
FLAKING OUT FOR VARIOUS REASONS
THE DOWNED HEDGE OF PROTECTION
THE WEAK ARE OUR BLOCK
MORAL INSANITY TAUGHT IN SCHOOLS
AWARENESS IS KEY TO GROWTH

GENIUS IS HELD DOWN:
Envy the Biggest Human Emotion

ALCOHOL KILLS FAMILIES
THE HEALING HOME
MISTREATMENT BRINGS GROWTH
BEST SAINTS WERE WORST SINNERS
TOO WEAK TO STAND UP FOR SELF
PEOPLE PLEASING SUPPRESSES EMOTIONS
THE TERRIBLE POSSESSION
BE YOUR OWN THERAPIST
MANY MORE OPPORTUNITIES
UNCONTROLLED RAGE OF WOMEN
NARCISSIST TACTICS INVOLVE OTHERS
RECORDING IN HEAD ENDURES
FILL THE HOLE WITH JESUS
REPENT FOR A PINK CLOUD THAT NEVER GOES AWAY
NO MORE FILLIN ARE YOU A VICTIM OR CHAMPION?
SO YOU MESSED UP, FORGET IT
AVOID NON-ESSENTIALITY
THE LESSON IS GRATITUDE
END CYCLES TO START NEW ONES
FOR BEAUTY/STYLE COME OUTA DENIAL
LIFE IS A STAIRS SO FORGET THE LOWER
LIBERTY = HAPPY
NO MORE FILLING TIME
BIGGEST ENEMIES ARE IN YOUR HOUSEHOLD
YOU WERE FRAMED
GOD RAISES ONE AND PUTS THE OTHER DOWN
THE SIN OF SLOTH
DIVINE APPOINTMENT: DO YOUR THING
SUPERIOR PEOPLE HAVE FEWEST FRIENDS

GENIUS IS HELD DOWN:
Envy the Biggest Human Emotion

REPENTANCE BRINGS BOLDNESS
BAD PAST ALL ERASED
IT WASN'T YOU BUT DEMONS COMING THROUGH
TURNING POINTS
SEE THINGS PROPHETICALLY
THE SAINTS ARE WISE AND WITTY
LOOKING BACK WE SEE DEMONS
TALK IS CHEAP
DON'T RESENT CONTROLLERS, TAKE CONTROL
SO MANY OPPORTUNITIES NOW
LIFE IS A PIE: DON'T WASTE TIME!
ELIMINATE TO EXPAND
RICHES CAN MAKE MISCHIEF
AVOID LOGORHEA AND MANY WORDS
THE FEELING OF GOING BEYOND
ANTICIPATE WHILE YOU WAIT
WITH GOD NO ONE'S STUCK
OVERCOME ENVY FOR SUCCESS
SELF-GENTLENESS IS KEY
DUNCES IN CONFEDERACY AGAINST
STAY WITH CONFIRMERS
DECIDE TO END YOUR REACTIONS
PLATITUDES TO AVOID JUDGMENT
MR. AND MRS. SMILEY
DON'T TRACK YOUR MIND
SWAMP UPDATES
NOT A NICKEL TO A LIBERAL
PUT ON THE NEW SELF
DETOX OR DIE

Notes to Champs

Any fool can know. The point is to understand. Albert Einstein.

OUR SELF IMAGE IS TRASHED EARLY

Our self-image is trashed early, determining all that we attract later to confirm that bad identity.

The smarter one is the more messed up they get when wires are crossed, hearts broken, rejected.

Cross a narcissist and it's their entire goal to hurt you as much as they can so don't get involved man.

Narcissists are scorekeepers. You got an edge so now he's gotta make things right--must sequester.

Vengeance is Mine--the Lord. God'll get em better than you ever could but He WILL only if you won't.

Give foe to God with grace, forgiveness, mercy and love and you're free: God goes on a killing spree.

Life is hell when attracting confirmers of a pre-existing identity by a mother who had jealous anger.

Stiff-necked and haughty—that's our persecutors until we see it's a chemical cue interactionally.

As a child it was "normal" which translates to "familiar" which means "safe" and so she was raped.

Familiarity meant she never heard insults. She was so used to her mother's she just tuned it all out.

GENIUS IS HELD DOWN

She felt safe with bad boys she let in to the horror of anyone with a brain seeing disaster coming.

She was so used to disaster/drunken brawls in the home she didn't even see catastrophe brewin'

It's about how certain societies/families make us mentally ill then it's contagious as hell.

ATTRACTING CONFIRMERS OF TRASHED IDENTITY

She attracted confirmation of the trashed identity by mean women friends calling her sweetie.

Her life up to old age was one big confirmation of the early trauma and they were all bad mama.

The brain is wired early, chaos/mixed signals are templated as safe and life is now a big pain.

Female genius is so maligned the only answer is to find one man's love and treat him like a god.

Don't marry a man who's social with porous boundaries, exposing you to hurt. It's solitude sir.

Jolly Jimmy demanded I let the world in and I entered hell as the hedge was down/I sunk in swill.

Don't wait until old age for a home behind a locked gate with a dedicated mate so happily alone ok.

Be selective, i.e. exclusive. I was degraded 20 years from Jolly Jimmy's demons from being inclusive.

MUST BE EXCLUSIVE AND SELECTIVE

When a trashed genius sees higher realities/how his was created by mommy/siblings--he's free.

GENIUS IS HELD DOWN

To attract the same sarcastic mocking your whole life is due to an early program in your biocomputer.

The women are the meanest. They've adapted one way and **HATE** those who won't, can't or resist.

To a rigid female conformist there's nothing more hideous/aggravating than a unique genius.

Even as a child I sensed women were mean and men were nice but even that was wires crossed.

With alcoholism, paganism or debauched liberalism in the other the identity/mirroring is disturbed.

FEMALE GENIUS IS RARE SIS

The potential for female genius--which is entirely unique or peculiar--is quickly thru conformity bashed.

The human biocomputer just assumes that if it is familiar it is safe, even a violent drunken rage.

Not only does she face female monsters on the outer, she has angry voices on the inner, yellers.

It's her template creating this weird world which she assumes to be universal--but it's not girl.

You let men in who were dangerous but seen as safe and that's why your life is hell on earth ok.

The damaged biocomputer thinks: I don't matter, my needs don't matter and I don't deserve better.

They can't figure her out. She's a dingbat, insane, criminal or a witch--whatever, just shut her up.

A male genius has his problems but females hardly exist--though the potential is there I insist.

GENIUS IS HELD DOWN

Two blueprints: One goes out attracted to those who cherish her, the other to users and losers.

The sick biocomputer is scared and unhappy due to the constant recreation of his early beginnings.

RETICULAR ACTIVATING SYSTEM

Our reticular activating system works with our beliefs to filter out information, thus repetition.

This system needs to narrow down all the information so we can survive in that particular ground.

The filter takes us thru life naturally gravitating to the familiar tho' they be destructive characters.

We are transformed by the renewal of our mind--then we stop picking those who ignore us, aye.

Gravitating to the familiar [TOXIC] relationship getting your blood boiling is a chemical reaction see.

There is a strong physiological/chemical reaction to soul ties--when chaos is her comfort zone, aye.

She thinks "why am I constantly attracting this?" It's normal not cuz she lost her "confidence".

It's how people with like backgrounds/culture "find" each other but it duplicates bad weather.

The brain can be rewired. From living out your old survival protocols to living free/speaking bold.

THE MISWIRED BRAIN IS ABOUT SURVIVAL

The only protocol a miswired brain has is survival in a densely-programmed system of lunatics, all.

GENIUS IS HELD DOWN

The brain is not wired to successfully "thrive" but in that crazy people world, just to keep you alive.

That's how powerful the survival mode is: the abnormal behavior blindly lasts forever unless resisted.

Take the pressure off yourself. You were simply living out the defective program to live, that's all.

Does rejection lead to emotional numbness? Such are longterm effects of manipulation/being dissed.

MISJUDGMENTS LOCKED IN MUSCLES

All their gripes and misjudgments are locked in your muscles and GSR, the galvanic skin response.

You reacted with anger and promptly blocked the response which locked in as present neuroses.

In a small liberal town i felt like a stranger in a strange land but in flyover country I'm happy man.

The pattern is the same. A trauma happens then they start to eat, drink, use and can't stop ok.

Is she bipolar or supersensitive, reacting to certain environments? I was the latter, misjudged.

A sick and debauched environment is also a mean place. Meanness and nastiness surely relate.

The victims of mean nastiness pass it on and it's horrible to realize you did this/were one.

Happy alone I felt sick around certain people. Was I bipolar or just supersensitive to evil?

Taking a systems view--extending it to the environment--abnormal behaviors make sense too.

GENIUS IS HELD DOWN

TO YOUR *NEW* NEURAL PATHWAYS

If you can't explain things simply then you don't understand them well enough. Albert Einstein

On miracles/synchronicity: coincidence is God's way of remaining anonymous. Albert Einstein

You're only old once so enjoy it to the max: your highest stage of optimum height of glory/apex.

Right when you're reached your glory crown they start to put you down tho' it's just a number man.

You grow up overcoming bad friends. Though they threw you bones see em as stepping stones.

Every bad relationship I suffered and overcame made me more creative and wise: total gains.

See it like that or sink in your swill of bad memories and resentments boiling you up/making you crazy.

A horrible guy who made me cry taught me a lesson so high: avoid anyone resembling him, aye.

WE GROW BY OVERCOMING BAD FRIENDS

You grow up overcoming bad friends. Though they threw you bones see em as stepping stones.

It wasn't such a bad day just you getting experience of what it's like being falsely accused ok.

It wasn't such a horrible phase just your Ph.D. in the Streets making you so smart you amaze.

Since you're only old once you should maximize this phase or bust [get decrepit/turn to dust].

GENIUS IS HELD DOWN

Looking back it isn't that you were immature but addicted and that makes us little kids.

Look at your sordid past as a trip you were on to teach you lessons the others are still stuck in.

Never let someone in only to be SHOCKED as they become dangerously confrontational.

Never get into a car only to be SHOCKED as they haul you around like cargo or they rage/mock.

SHOCKED BY FLIP-FLOPS

Your days of being SHOCKED as they flip scripts from nice to brash/helpful to ruinous are over sis.

For man has two sides/two separate nervous systems--even the nice ones all have a tiger in em.

Edacity--wanting to devour everything in sight--comes from trauma and mishandling of emotions.

I made gold on edacity and became a mini-faster instead, it's hard getting me to eat in fact.

All I knew was I was only happy eating, or my emotions would rose up against me/it was terrifying.

This was an unconscious state and I was full of denial about it. Fasting once, this all changed up.

From mindless eating to preferring the great results of fasting and learning from mistakes digesting.

FORGET DETAILS: THROW THE BAG OUT

It's too taxing going thru every memory of a decades long mental illness--put it all in a bag to go out.

GENIUS IS HELD DOWN

Chalk it up to false accusation as they made a big deal outa nothing and besides you're repenting.

What woman hasn't felt sized up by a female--looking you up and down more than males?

Women leaving husbands for greener pastures cuz they want sex with someone else/devil's lure.

LOSING THE HEDGE OF PROECTION

It's not so much that the world is against you--which it is--but due to sins you lost your hedge.

Give up silliness and practical jokes. They're both outa grace so lead to much greater dangers folks.

Don't let time freeze your mind. The past when viewed from present perspectives seems so unkind.

She stands against domestic violence but the feminist world hates her for taking on Johnny giant.

A true feminist would take a stand against famous men but that's only when they're God's friends.

These so-called feminists are just as much into hero-worship and are thus air-heads and twits.

The abuser always demands you burn your bridges behind you so he can start attacking too.

A narcissist can't allow tranquility and peace. He must win though there's no competition in place.

I thought feminists supported abused women--but if the husband's a movie star they side with him?

Wife of the alcoholic takes on blame and bad identity and even sucks up for his approval honey.

GENIUS IS HELD DOWN

SEEKING APPROVAL OF RASCALS

They love outsiders more than insiders and that's a TRAITOR. Multicultural: America killers.

She reminded me of a square jawed female Nazi prison guard--tough feminists to be feared.

The alcoholic slips into ultra-respect for authority figures--anyone in control they bow before.

In every dam case in which she was gotten drunk and raped she was made to feel to blame ok?

The saints have remorse for their sins, that's what distinguishes them from the common.

I'm so creative when I'm loved/not being abused. Make hay while the sun shines to be the muse.

The more insane, lunatic, ridiculous and outrageous you were the more you're a miracle, adored.

Mom/Dad are eternally grateful I brought em to Jesus and angels but I feel shame for being awful.

IT FEELS LIKE ETERNAL GUILT

At least I have a conscience that hasn't been seared like everyone else: callous messes/debauched.

Men don't like being chased. A lady/queen never chases a man. Her pleading devalues her SMV.

I refuse the hero worship surrounding you. The gopher suckup sycophants and flying monkeys too.

It wasn't an overnight success. It' just blossomed suddenly after fifty years I confess.

GENIUS IS HELD DOWN

Daily work and routine, tenacity and some audacity and the result with years was completion see.

I built an electronic Taj Mahal that's all, a huge place reflecting how I see the world/it's a ball.

It wasn't that you were a rascal/donkey's ass but a weak vessel so Satan's demons had the edge.

Don't worry: past foes are either dead, in jail or toothless grifters fighting you to no avail.

Sorry to tell you all this bad stuff about human nature but you knew it all anyway didn't ya?

RECAP/THOUGHTS ON THE GREAT WORK

Most are younger and don't know what I'm talking about so let music be the voice and bell ringer.

I feel like God designed it all and it's my job to find it. I don't claim credit for any of it, I love Him.

When a Creative Act--a structure in nature--is complete it attracts pollination, e.g. like a rich Arabian.

People were far smarter a century ago. Intentionally we're made as dumb as rocks ya' know.

Most southern California desert towns are meth places now. Stealin' and dealin' is their motto.

I'm so glad to be outa California. The people here are so normal after all that-- mal-adapting to mania.

We create thru ELIMINATION, not addition. That's just superfluity: learn to prune your stuff honey.

Desert Movie is called "All Uphill Now": we've released obstructions and recovered from the fall.

GENIUS IS HELD DOWN

It wasn't so much that I was terrible and awful but that alcohol's a conduit to the devil and hell.

For the Hero's Path is circuitous and thorny at times, I've been down in dirty street grime but overcame it all, aye.

The completion of the Creative Act attracts pollination--that's your link hon' so just relax/party on.

Butter with potatoes is a cement block that takes forever to get out: food combining by Kellock.

I don't find it offensive, I love Jesus whether I listen to world chillout beat or not so I resist this.

Evil globalists control mass migratory flow. Push it here, create food crisis there, put out the lure.

Democrat party supported the Clan, slavery, Jim Crow and segregation but we're to blame man.

GENIUS IS HELD DOWN:
Envy the Biggest Human Emotion

The mental disease of the century is narcissistic sociopathy manifested in having no empathy.

When you move to the desert for solitude and instead meet a tidal wave of small town RUDE.

Why did I so want solitude? Like Plato said no one's more hated than he who speaks the truth.

Narcissist abuse isn't just about pretty people. She can be unpretty but still a danger to you lady.

It doesn't mean sister abuse doesn't exist just cuz Carol Burnette did a comic skit on it you twit.

I'm writing about a rotting hole in my gut and a dark cloud over my thoughts for decades.

Now women are cruel to each other, they hold each other down, sister jealousy's full blown.

THE PAST AS A DOC ON YOU

Instead of embarrassment of the past just think of it as a documentary on you with good reviews.

Think of it as a documentary filled with good comments justifying all your mistakes tho' evil.

Tho' Joplin made an ass of herself in '65 the comments now cover everything over and she's fine.

Instead of describing utter depravity of your sins they just say "she was derailed for a while then".

GENIUS IS HELD DOWN

The past is kind in other words, and if they hear how bad you really are they think: falsehood.

If you're good now the crowd will turn against your degrader for saying such awful things about her.

If I think of paradise--gorgeous scenes all around, God's beauty & bounty--I'm happy but people, angry.

I'm the happiest I've ever been with you not around friend so we know why I was crazy then.

Sibling abuse is an uphill climb. It feels like we're climbing a mountain so exhausted, aye.

All I did was defend myself, having no energy left for what I do best as secret hostilities I sensed.

Detachment means peace of mind. We don't wanna be stuck in toxicity, we want to expand see.

Old toxic dynamics and false belief systems no more: we wanna transform, metamorphize, soar.

I got so used to hate & secrecy surrounding me I sunk in my swill crying, drinking, seeking sympathy.

SISTER ABUSE

Sister abuse is an uphill battle since you're never truly free until you're out of the family jungle.

She's an expert at sly, subtle shit-shots about your character. You're no match, being introvert.

She's an expert at getting on the horn and destroying you on your throne. Prepare to be gone.

They assumed the "big sister" was correct about me since she was older, what vicious deceit.

GENIUS IS HELD DOWN

While under her tyranny she controlled me solely through gossipping on the phone see.

Everyone she talked with turned against me. I was going crazy but never pinned it on Big Sis see.

It's these weak, secret, underhanded tactics jezebels and female narcs use: hardly a muse.

Suddenly, when you were minding your own business, you're in a heap of trouble caused by sis.

If there's attorneys involved she'll get to them first, priming them against you, the family curse.

UNREALIZED JEALOUSY

I was nervous, unhappy, scared all the time. A knot in my gut, how could these be sisters of mine?

I encountered the same type of jealous hostility from girls in school. They were real bullies too.

I always reacted to jealous hostility by sucking up more see until I understood the whole scene.

Jealousy: the biggest human emotion leads to murder often. That in essence is what you're facin'.

She didn't murder you but tried to get you locked up which would have been tantamount.

It was all necessary for your development: ups, downs, reversals, faux pas, insults, disappointments.

The female community is a massive impediment to genius--they put you down and it's callous.

She can't trust females, it's all envy/hostility. She can't trust males, all they want is sex presumably.

GENIUS IS HELD DOWN

Her "male friends" are usually betas, bad advice comes from them in America, it's female hysteria.

ATTEMPTING TO BE SOCIAL? WHY

I was always too inner driven and introverted to ever have a social life, it is only pure boredom.

I wanted to write, they sought to relate. I was bothered by the rinky dink and just wanted to think.

To fully realize genius she has to conquer loneliness and enjoy solitude. Work in silence: seclude.

If she's attempting to be social she'll lose her role as lightning rod: catalyst, muse for y'all.

Unbelievably, people wanna be close to their neighbors and even live in cities. This is funny to me.

I bought two acres next to me JUST for the buffer zone between me and human unpredictability.

EVERY DAY SELF-CHOSEN

Now every day's a self-chosen paradise. I am NEVER in reaction and the day is mine without surprises.

A billionaire always directs his own day and never reacts to droppers in, no way! Copy this now ok.

Never let em use you as entertainment. They're bored and lonely, you're not and very busy tell em.

People are desperately bored and lonely so come to you baby and then you're their slave surely.

You're up early, working energetically, enthusiastically and free--then they come to derail thee.

GENIUS IS HELD DOWN

Satan is there to block your plans and he uses people obviously, the weak vessels you have around.

Office Hours means: NO interruptions and no one ever comes even your own husband or son.

Hero's Path begins bothersome with many obstacles to overcome then its perfection: you've won.

It's not a vain habit but a fatal mental illness. Think like that before you criticize her highness.

My life is easy now in contrast to the onerousness of my having to fight dense resistances all around.

If no built boundaries your life will be hell as water seeks its own level and it all flows in: evil.

To me family meant dyads, triads, interlocking jealousy patterns, mixed signals, secrecy, treachery.

All I knew was the gut-wrenching petty competition and sterile inhumane dynasties I was fightin'

They were liars and cheats basically, with a facade of goodness and success that was hypnotizing.

It was so ridiculous how long I put up with it and so relieving to finally boldly stand up to it.

As you see miracles come together in a pattern you learn to love doing God's work/exciting.

LIBERAL LIARS AND CHEATS

Racial quotas are not victimless crimes. Many are qualified but you're shutting out the prime.

We are stepping backward into unconstitutional racism and it's ugly: skin color gets you goodies.

GENIUS IS HELD DOWN

The truckers are the first hope we've had. What a brilliant idea, we Americans are so glad!

Saying we're the bad guys when all we want is to live our lives, free of encroachment/evil ties.

Liberalism meant freedom in the sixties but now it means tyranny you see in your siblings.

Their arguments make no sense as their position is indefensible, even yelling "racist" to the lovable.

Emotion wells up in me then when I work it out in a two-liner I understand it all and it's now ok.

IF YOU WANT IT YOU AIN'T GETTING IT

Narc: "If you want it, you ain't getting it". He appears at the last minute, he gives just enough.

To save sanity you must recognize disrespect when you see it. Stop trying to make it right/reject it.

Let go of partial solutions and disrespect making room for an expert with success you can expect.

They promise then they withhold. The more they know you want it the more the answer is NO.

One begins to show the effects of a sick love relationship: come here, go away.

Whether in a personal or business relationship these cycles will make you sick, blocked, wrecked.

SICKLY CYCLICITY

The effects of sickly cyclicity: what the nervous system can take before your creativity is sacked.

Sick addiction to the bad source: when he appears there's so much relief you forget the curse.

GENIUS IS HELD DOWN

One begins to show the effects of a sick love relationship: come here, go away quick.

Show up, do splendid work, solve problems. Disappear, ghost, refuse to answer, let it go altogether.

These inconsistent cycles drive the human biocomputer MAD. There are sick geniuses, it's a fact.

Energy thieves make promises, withhold, give just enough, show up at late then bring relief.

It gives you hope to know creating a space will bring in your Ace, that one God chose for your case.

The energy thief eventually brings your relief because that keeps you in the ring endlessly.

He may hate you but he needs you so there's gotta be something he can do to be that glue.

The energy thief eventually brings your relief because that keeps you endlessly in the ring.

If you don't see cycles of those in your employment you're driven mad just like any sick relationship.

In this thorny situation your self-esteem and even your purpose is held hostage by an inferior.

An inferior you depend upon and trust who's acting like this will degrade the work, a hit and miss.

OBVIOUS DISRESPECT

There's no respect and it's obvious. it's you who's oblivious and that's the problem miss.

The effects of sickly cyclicity: what the nervous system can take before it sacks all creativity.

GENIUS IS HELD DOWN

I felt the effects of a sick relationship, evoking memories of similar feelings/disappointments.

I'd retire before working with inferior workers. Never again: clouds without rain, shirkers.

Even if he eventually shows up you've gotta take care of yourself and recognize he should be out.

Even if you forsake a project you'll feel much better with him gone forever--it was gloomy weather.

For if you don't forsake it--at least with him—you're his hostage and definitely on the begging end.

The world is filled with em. Even if talented they have poor character and true respect is rare.

Ending a disrespectful relationship is like removing a nail from your foot after all the crap you took.

As long as there's a glimmer of hope you're still a hostage. End it anyway and you'll de-age.

It's affected your health. You can't live in a vacillating environment without exhaustion/giving up.

FLAKING OUT FOR VARIOUS REASONS

People flake out for various reasons. Drugs, alcohol, sexual liaisons. Whatever, they've changed.

All hep on his morals one day, narcissist rewrites script the next and accepts it all as all-ok.

Whatever you've been putting up with/going blind to is unqueenly and it degrades your looks too.

So cut your losses and get out now. You didn't need it anyway, you'll attract new work pals.

GENIUS IS HELD DOWN

Cut him loose and self-respect creeps back. You'll feel happy again after your world went black.

If one mistreats you it's not of God. Take the hint and move on, hold your head high with aplomb.

THE DOWNED HEDGE OF PROTECTION

Life ran smoothly [humming] but with sin thorny and difficult [grating]: note the two states honey.

It's not that you're mad at fifty people but that era was sinful making people problems inevitable.

When in sin God removes the Hedge of Protection, evil streams in and you may welcome it even.

Sin brings bad associations causing other problems and you spiral down from there, amen.

Thank you Michelle for teaching me all about Jezebels and to never lend anything to that girl.

Is that how you treat a mentally ill person? He's crazy in the head that's why he acts so dumb.

THE WEAK ARE OUR BLOCK

Lord, what they put me through. But we won't talk about that anymore: the bitter pills I had to swallow.

You think you got family but in the end they screw you too. Sopranos

"The weak can never forgive. Forgiveness is the attribute of the strong." ~ Mahatma Gandhi

When a wife gets more beautiful it's because her husband makes her happy--or very unhappy.

Any loner/black sheep knows they've been talking--the grapevine ebbs and flows, sickening.

GENIUS IS HELD DOWN

Be on guard at all times and never give in--and most of all, watch your bad associations.

I don't know what made me so mentally ill. A combo of extreme stress, trauma, malnutrition, Obama.

People are so cruel it's better to commiserate with the world since they've been abused too girl.

I am sorry to tell you these things and smash your sacred cows but that's how it goes to be a rose.

I hated being on the wrong side of God. It went on for decades that painful wheel for new pots.

It's like the more pain the more gain. The more potential the more painful the path for the disciple.

I grimace at bad memories but then I think of WWII and the holocaust and see my molehill was tiny.

The natural tendency is to *get back*. But they're dead, in a rest home or have no memory of the facts.

We've all done crazy evil stuff too, in blind ignorance or moral insanity but God forgave us totally.

MORAL INSANITY TAUGHT IN SCHOOLS

99% of moral insanity was actually taught in the schools so it was easy for us to become fools.

Moral insanity taught and advanced in the schools put us in a fog [being false] and in sin [what else].

The biological instincts--sex and food--are the first to warp from these sick cultural influences.

It's ALL about sex and their genitals, I kid you not! It should all be about growing more into God.

GENIUS IS HELD DOWN

Ultimately you just have to eat crow and forgive em. Think of all you did in a complete fog hon'

How many times did you screw up, cover it up, act like it never happened or try not to think about it?

I'm not saying forget it because non-Christians have no lines but it helps in dividing/saying goodbye.

The devil gets ahold of us especially if alcohol's involved. You become less careless with age--strong.

How to change your people-pleasing and attention-seeking behavior: get a life in the INNER.

Why we tend to attract mates who are emotionally unavailable and then act out, horrible.

In my experience coming from a dysfunctional household, I was a people-pleaser and not at all bold.

I was a people pleaser so they wouldn't hit me or like me a little better but inside was a fester.

Because they didn't respect me for my people-pleasing especially since I was miserable, totally.

AWARENESS IS KEY TO GROWTH

Had I known then what I know now: That I just wanna be in my own home with every minute my own.

People are cruel and the sooner you get walled in the better--and women, don't be degraded further.

Don't let men expect perverted six acts from you--don't give in to the perv culture taught in the schools.

For these things are totally degrading to you as a child of God. Think of everything your Father saw.

GENIUS IS HELD DOWN

ALCOHOL KILLS FAMILIES

We had a good marriage, we were friends, we built things so why did it tragically end? alcohol, amen.

Just one drink and he was an all-day wino. It was like lighting a fire and he descended into hell.

Because it was genetic, one drink and I lost my husband to the terrible addiction which killed him.

One drink, that's all it takes to light that fire and I'm including cough/NyQuil or wine with dinner.

How to deal with toxic memories: Realize that's what it took to get the highest blend in a mind/body.

I'd wake up after drinking the night before HORRIFIED at what I had said/did, it was so out of character.

So I'd resume drinking--hair of the dog--to deal with these unacceptable memories, that's all.

It's been 30 years without a drop and every day's happy unless it's a person here bothering me.

THE HEALING HOME

I can't believe I spent time/energy trying to get their approval when all I had to do was stay home.

The past was like a bow and arrow: I was pulled WAY WAY, WAY back to go WAY, WAY, WAY forward.

The more back, the more forward. The best saints really WERE the worst sinners, the lessons were hard.

Mom used to say: Why you keep going out? Just stay home, that's where it's all at. That's a fact.

MISTREATMENT BRINGS GROWTH

GENIUS IS HELD DOWN

It was hell on earth being mistreated/used by people but that was the lesson pushing me up the hill.

You have no idea how creepy people can be when they don't respect you. I've seen it/noted it too.

They like you since you'll do their bidding/do favors but they don't respect you as a person for it.

I don't wanna attract people who use me. I've had it with that and will run the other way or lock the gate.

It's exhausting to be a people pleaser and a hellish life. That's enough motivation to end this strife.

Instead of resentment at memories, put your thoughts on the growth--social muscle--from the tragedy.

Anyone wanting privacy, asking em to leave or call first will be treated as a hater and even inferior.

BEST SAINTS WERE WORST SINNERS

The great blessings I have today are from what I've overcome yesterday, that's what I say.

I climbed the highest mountain and I won the war. Maybe my words will be read when I'm gone more.

Being the worst sinners they had more gratitude for His rescue--that made em the greatest saints too.

I've had people disrespect me so much they awoke me at midnight to fix them a meal. I did it like a fool.

TOO WEAK TO STAND UP FOR SELF

I know how much it hurts being too weak to stand up for yourself against absurd demands, oh man...

GENIUS IS HELD DOWN

And then to get drunk to release the pressure, blow up for once, then cow-tow again from the shame.

I've had women visit me and ask to borrow things or use the computer. This is bad: low, brazen, clutter.

Some mental diseases cluster with others: Bulimia, kleptomania, promiscuity, hatred, etcetera.

The more they disrespect you for cow-towing the more absurd their demands and then you're dead.

The other negative of people pleasing is neglecting your own needs and ultimately hating yourself.

PEOPLE PLEASING SUPPRESSES EMOTIONS

To be a people-pleaser I had to suppress my emotions and this was an atom bomb on my system.

Locking away your emotions to adapt to that rat will cause cancer and other debilitating diseases: fact.

Heart disease and obviously anxiety and depression goes WAY up when you're suppressing to adapt.

You are literally destroying your body suppressing your emotions in favor of their emotions.

Triggers: I'd break into people pleasing when they were standoffish, ignoring or plain didn't like me.

Triggers are important cuz we can't fix a behavior not on the surface. Triggers flush em out to extinguish.

THE TERRIBLE POSSESSION

Many were possessed with the devil for decades--think what they have to deal with in memories.

GENIUS IS HELD DOWN

God brought you outa this mess--much being genetically determined--so ask Him to remove memories.

Possessed for decades, once "he's" out why go back and investigate any part of it? Be happy/forget it.

Did you know: more than hating you for your sins they hate you cuz you changed from what you'd been?

Therapy is simply responding to the triggers in a safe setting so the memories are re-ordered.

Without therapy, give yourself that empathy. You can re-route painful memories by this self-loving.

BE YOUR OWN THERAPIST

When someone's rude/disrespectful instead of breaking into people pleasing I simmer, ruminating.

WHY did I attract this, WHY would I want this. Not what can I do to *change* this to end the mess.

Instead of people pleasing, think: I'm worth more than this. I'm better than this/they're rinky dink.

Your inner child cries out for validation/acceptance but your adult walks that back to self-love instead.

You give yourself the love and empathy you lacked as a child. You become what you needed.

So you can change and manipulate those memories within you so that your life is joyous, like a child.

The memories were made in a different context--with lowlifes around--but now it's you, the best.

After therapy or self-empathy the triggers start to turn down and we don't react like that, a clown.

GENIUS IS HELD DOWN

No, I'm not gonna people please. My feelings are valid and I'm just gonna express em without pity.

When you stop PPing you're no longer attracted to emotionally unavailable people--how novel.

MANY MORE OPPORTUNITIES

When you heal there's no attraction to cold when there's so many who can love you back: the gold.

Attention-seeking is natural but if emotionally neglected it radically warps in ways you never expected.

We start seeking attention in negative ways, like acting out to get it. Disease and insanity gets it.

To correct your neurotic desire for attention, give others attention--it works like magic in a minute man.

Reduce attention-seeking behaviors by being creative, turning inward--losing respect for the herd.

Outward: I feel abandoned, act out. Inward: My attention i on my art and there's none of these thoughts.

When you start getting healthy attention the negative goes away. The triggers dissolve, ok?

There are many around just to take from you. Those will disappear now, aligned with a higher crew.

UNCONTROLLED RAGE OF WOMEN

I have faced the uncontrolled rage of women many times and tho' I forgave em I just never saw em again.

Who are they kidding? Feminists don't care about sexual assaults on women, they want **NO PRISON**.

GENIUS IS HELD DOWN

They'd rather have you dead, having made **NO** mark on the earth, of no influence forever, cursed.

It was always the same pattern: Whenever I adapt to lowlifes I become the worst of the lot, amen.

Your environment--the people you hang around--affect your identity and purpose, don't chance it.

If they don't edify you in the things of God, but tempt you to slip down, it's best to love em from a distance.

Walk with the wise and become wise for a companion of fools suffers harm. Prov. 13: 20

The righteous choose friends very carefully for the way of the wicked leads them astray. Prov 12: 26

The wicked are slaves to sin but the righteous are slaves to God—to that crucial difference, be awed.

What fellowship does light have with darkness? We should represent Christ in words and actions.

A Christian is very careful to not allow people to influence us--whether Christian or non-Christian sis.

NARCISSIST TACTICS INVOLVE OTHERS

Narcissistic abuse is not one-on-one as the narc gets the entire community involved to do his bidding.

The narcissist's tactics are often covert, and the only reason he's gossiping is to "help" not hurt her.

The victim of narc abuse is inculcated with learned helplessness and is frozen in defenselessness.

The victim has flashbacks/intrusive memories in addition to panic attacks depleting all his energy.

GENIUS IS HELD DOWN

Victim feels shame, depression, anxiety, embarrassment, humiliation. abandonment and vulnerability.

She deals with her abuser by internalizing him who becomes a voice in her head, an introject.

I was stalking myself with a ghost agent, my abuser--but I was the one with the memory-killers.

RECORDING IN HEAD ENDURES

Long after the divorce the victim continues to abuse herself by all the recordings in her head.

She constantly hears threats he made, challenges to her self-esteem, gaslighting, reality distortion.

All these inputations from the narc alien forms a composite picture to her of a grasshopper.

This negative self-image is from the repeated element with outcomes just like narcissistic stalking.

Since mistreatment brings such exquisite growth we should thank God for it-- can you believe it?

FILL THE HOLE WITH JESUS

The hole inside is only filled by Jesus Christ. You can talk to Him because He is alive.

View, music, bible, dictionary, dogs--what else would you need? Just these and my mind is freed.

You've been taught not to stereotype. But you can, with them—can't you see they're a blight?

They had class at first when they were high on he hog, but after their fall no one would applaud.

GENIUS IS HELD DOWN

Dogs have angels in them, it's a trade-off: The more you love the more they protect, what a payoff.

Leave me alone honey I just wanna study and though it doesn't mean money it's still my calling.

Mature aging is inner not outer so stop trying to fit silly crowds who only socialize with others.

One benefit of the Cinderella Syndrome is after marrying Prince he handles the sisters: awesome.

True genius is unique and we all have it: like a lost art unappreciated in the generation we're in (fact).

REPENT FOR A PINK CLOUD THAT NEVER GOES AWAY

You do live in a cornucopia after repentance: a pink cloud that never goes away--let it be today.

The sick family needs one onto whom they project their shadow cuz we're all sinners, kiddo.

Family divisions manifest in crisis but especially in reading the will as evil members meddle.

They will hate, scorn, mock and spread falsehoods about you: God's genius tool, which are few.

Cinderella Syndrome: Dissolve the template by holding your head up high and telling the truth.

Systems Therapy: "these are my enemies: my sisters and their progeny who hate me--an anomaly".

A woman can and should change a man. There's nothing wrong with that--it's God's Plan.

Recall our slogan: evil always meddles. Trust no man/read all contracts whether family or fellows.

GENIUS IS HELD DOWN

The bible is a history of God's intervention in the affairs of man over many centuries span.

Nobody knows who I am: If you're the outcast you're only a legend--hated but never mentioned.

Cure for friends/family of liberals: Stop fighting back and give it all to God who knows you're right, in fact.

ARE YOU A VICTIM OR CHAMPION?

Forget family annals from the past. Don't take victim status for you're a great champion at last!

I'm not sick I'm sensitive. There's a big difference but when in reaction I'm sick and never pensive.

Being single is having no walls as the outside world flows in. It means having no protection.

It's not that we "hate sin" but we hate what God hates and love what He loves: doves.

Put your writing first: take paper and pen on your walks. Don't lose as you did in the past, a lot.

Just be your unique creative genius self. Ignore all else but God and nature as the magic elf.

Chemicals cause emotional debasement not just on the physical level--we get evil and fickle.

They triggered his alcohol relapse with a bribe of 5 grand from my account then he died of drinking bout.

Virtually all freeway accidents are pile-ups. Bang,bang as they slam--slow down and pull back, Sam.

I don't keep money separate from my husband nor did we get a pre-nup--these aren't marriage/love.

GENIUS IS HELD DOWN

You create your dog's heath and temperament. He's putty in your hands so stop being negligent.

If I sense they've been primed against me I seek their approval on my knee-- how neurotic, gee.

I repent for every sin up to this moment. Start me over Lord: mend our connection broken.

SO YOU MESSED UP, FORGET IT

So you messed up, forget it. Pray God will repair and perfect the incident in mind: He will do it.

Black holes suck things IN, so deliberately refuse to feel offense and fly WAY above her or him.

Students report emotional crises and many seem fragile. We give into neurosis though it's God's battle.

The way he drives is unfair to the rider and that is the only definition of a good or bad driver.

Cast out all superfluity and non-essentiality: Go lite to be ready for changes overnight.

Shut up. If you clutter with words they miss the main points: If you over-talk you just annoy.

Stop obscuring main points with your gibberish. Yak yak, socializing and ego is so boring.

Chit-chat obscures main points. Stop talking about yourself and stick to the business.

When in important meetings stick to main points. Stop silly anecdotes, they disappoint.

AVOID NON-ESSENTIALITY

GENIUS IS HELD DOWN

Your only problem is superfluous words. Cut the pork and then edit it well-- reduce by thirds.

You're filled with superfluity and non-essentiality and that is your whole problem: obstruction.

Non-essential words, anecdotes, jocularity: these detract from who you are so please stick to facts.

It's not your main points but non-essential words. Stop littering when true meaning is preferred.

What obstructs: mindless talking. What you do about it: Go into solitude to enjoy life with out faking.

I changed my name and culture but then through the years got to know dead ancestors: the Kellock sirs.

THE LESSON IS GRATITUDE

The lesson is gratitude for what you do have not yearning for what you don't: Christian path.

He's had to handle platoons of men, that's why he yells. So I was told by my gentle uncles.

When you change, your dogs do immediately. That's how finely attuned as you both fight the enemy.

Music solves all of your problems in mind, whereas TV tracks it into chaos and the same old grind.

Through 30 years in the wilderness with medical cannabis I found destiny then love and happiness.

We all makes mistakes but repentance is all it takes to get right again and stop being flakes.

A well-developed female side doesn't make a man effeminate but charming, artsy and adamant.

GENIUS IS HELD DOWN

If you get too close to them their little lives and inner fights take you over--not too clever!

We get so angry we may explode on those closest. Recall: anger is cuz we know the most.

I know the Lord, you only know the world. Get away from me you gofer sycophants/slow turtles.

Give people money: some will kill themselves with it but wise others will only increase it.

Multiple chemical sensitivities is also sensitivity to pain--from what I've been through I think it's the same.

END CYCLES TO START NEW ONES

It is always depressing when an old worn-out cycle ends but soon your new life begins and you win.

Even the best of boob jobs creates multiple chemical sensitivities within five years plus many tears.

They fall to the side, they get in the way, they hurt. She was glad to be rid of them and became so alert.

We all get chemically zapped but it's far less probable on a thousand acres or with air filters.

I feel so much more elegant now without those gross things. What a relief as my soul sings!

Being in solitude you're on top of the world--you see everything--but being enmeshed, nothing.

If it's important, by all means say it: speak! But if it's not please be silent so I can finally think!

Here I thought we were months away and it all happened in a day. God works fast if you pray.

GENIUS IS HELD DOWN

Just because you think it doesn't mean you should say it so please shut up so I can create it.

How the male-female thing works: God puts a bee in my bonnet then I get my smart husband on it.

Sabbath Blessing: May the reality of Jesus strike you with awe and a fresh sense of wonder!

MCS patients must be doctors with out diplomas to keep doctors from killing them with ego/ignorance.

FOR BEAUTY/STYLE COME OUTA DENIAL

What uglifies and ages us the most is unrecognized or unrepentant sins--being a trash bin.

At first she was beautiful and dapper--chic. But years later she was fat, dumb and up a creek.

It doesn't happen at first, the changes are incremental through the years. Sin degrades body/brings tears.

It's true that in those years I did go insane but it was all from adapting to Grace Ann and Jane.

I'm not a sitting duck for controllers anymore, I've got a husband to protect me: this is freedom--family.

Don't worry because He's the alpha and omega, the beginning and the end--relax friends, amen.

Every so often, clear the decks. Return to silence and sweet solitude--remove the hex.

Within five years of a boob job you will have Multiple Chemical Sensitivities (MCS)--really.

The job of the poet is making clear the words of the tribe. Loose ends come together: imbibe.

GENIUS IS HELD DOWN

The years went by but still I'm your girl and you're my guy. How wonderful you make it to be alive.

Sailing through the backcountry after navigating the city. SO relieved to get back, giddy.

If it's important by all means say it! But if not, shut up because all it does is block thought!

I know you wanna sing, but honey I gotta think and it's like being shot when you block thoughts.

Goal: To become rich through the work you love after deciding what is best with God above.

I'm not alone anymore. I was a sitting duck before, like I had a bull's eye painted on me—it was war!

My dogs like music not the news and other chaos. As a good mother that's what I choose most.

A divine gravitic pull keeps you tightly aligned with God. No more upsets though they'll call you odd.

Suspicious of anything natural/made by God. Accepting of what's made by man no matter how odd

We now have "antibiotic injury lawyers". I knew it and always refused to take them as they are cripplers.

LIFE IS A STAIRS SO FORGET THE LOWER

Stop thinking of your past/lower levels of consciousness. Life is like stairs so stay high like a priestess.

When God gives up He gives you up to sin and you're swooped into a giant trash bin separated from kin.

It's a wave that hits me: of acid, nausea and vertigo. Then I gotta get away and I'm all-ok, like presto.

GENIUS IS HELD DOWN

One who everyone loved/the most popular turned out to be the creepiest. Alone, she dissolved like a pest.

I'm afraid of disorder, to me it's the devil. Dirty chaos reflects a mind in trouble and it's lower than animals.

Look at your history as all-good cuz it got you here. Mine it for wisdom then have good cheer!

LIBERTY = HAPPY

You are the God Who does wonders: You have demonstrated Your power among all the peoples.

God actually changes a bad memory into a good one. He even changes the act itself, though it was done.

That's all behind you now. You've paid your dues, you lived the blues but now you are renowned.

Facing death brings transformation of reality. Then God saves and you become yourself, truly.

Optimize results by doing less. Maximize by cutting back and reducing stress. Relax: no mess.

The less you do the more you'll get done. Let the unconscious take hold and fall into place: you've won.

Let it percolate, distill the thought. Don't rush, have patience, let it unfold and you'll get the gold pot.

I've gotta stop somewhere so it may as well be here. This is enough to chew on, have no fear.

Do your best work by starting your party. R and R releases completion and they'll call you smarty.

in fighting against being lazy you got too busy. Bcuz the small things you missed being so fussy.

GENIUS IS HELD DOWN

Your silliness makes big mistakes. Delete this unnecessary drivel for world success, you flakes!

Realize it was demons: It happens! As you look back that should explain it all, bringing balance.

Hit me and I'll hit you back twice as hard. Be sweet and I'm your best friend: the bard.

Age has nothing to do with maturity. Very few are mature if it doesn't happen early.

This is what I had to endure to get to here. But I learned to love it anyway, and not to fear:

I'm like Drudge--I use one picture. No selfies here, it's about the inner.

NO MORE FILLING TIME

Filling time, I go to sleep. But just sitting looking out the window it's so intense, energizing/deep.

Can't track movies anymore, just music and travel logs.

The cure for the present is to explore the past.

Even music became too much--bird recordings only, in all rooms.

For 30 years, a tiny cabin in desert wilderness. Coulda gone to Europe but this built greater finesse.

Pamela Geller's job is to report bad news so she watches old movies to compensate for the blues.

Facebook is: planting seeds for future reactions.

If you don't like it don't come here.

We went to the shelter and brought home a darling little monster who changed our lives forever.

GENIUS IS HELD DOWN

They take em back like they don't work then by the 3rd pet adopter they've gone berserk.

Everything we eat our dogs wanna--just check it out first, please. Stick to a schedule, so they know/are pleased

It's Sunday and we're not supposed to work. Just look out the window, pray and read God's word.

The highest therapies are scientifically: pets, music (and looking out the window for me).

What a Sunday I had yesterday, looking out the window all afternoon and I'm doing the same thing today.

Be strong. If animals or kids sense weakness they tend to abuse and that describes the human throng.

BIGGEST ENEMIES ARE IN YOUR HOUSEHOLD

A man's biggest enemies are in his own household. That the bible says clearly and it's bold.

A breach of trust is a literal wound in the psyche--just seeing them brings revulsion, yikes.

When the wicked rule the people mourn. Daily trauma having a bad parent: wishing you were never born.

When a hero falls the whole gang gets in on the archetypal punishment for failing to be King.

The hero goes through phases--like scorn followed by complete solitude in the desert wilderness.

See yourself in the context of the system (rejected), then see yourself as free (elected)!

To adapt to hate she used a palliative--sin--but that brought more excruciating hate and no friends.

GENIUS IS HELD DOWN

Give her something she's never had: dignity, appreciation, respect, you--and you'll say "how she grew".

Justice is one of God's attributes. You wanna see them get their's otherwise life has no meaning/fruits.

You gotta know who you are. And that they depend on you staying high/pure as their only exemplar.

The godly home is filled with treasures. These homes attract what they are: joy beyond measure.

Being faithful is not about "him" but me. It's God I'm being faithful to, a covenant not free.

A short fuse reflects bad memories locked inside. Gotta get it all out then just ride the tide.

With so much old baggage there's nothing we can do right. We're out of grace, a blight.

His dad whipped him daily all through his teens. It's locked in the system and that's why he's mean.

Due to past trauma we expected nothing but bad. But we're on a magic carpet ride now, so glad!

A good man: does everything he says he'll do and everything he predicts comes true.

From every window it's exquisite and every day I thank God for it and also: I can't wait to share it.

I just wanna live here with you. To mutually appreciate every nook/cranny and the fabulous view.

If I stay home all the time that means happy creative safe days all the time, a lesson learned in my prime.

YOU WERE FRAMED

GENIUS IS HELD DOWN

You frame people by "framing" them: seeing them in a certain light, as an underling or a mere thing.

Something stinks and you don't know what--somethings unfolding here and it's the same old rut.

Be a legend to yourself. So what if they can't see you, beautifully designed by God and cute too.

Your taste and style is inborn, man. Very few have it but if you do just get into it--expand.

There's a mentally ill "bug": hyper-sensitives so very touchy but really, they just need a hug.

If your way is better, show them! For we all die soon and this is your time: it has come.

I don't let it go to my head cuz I know God giveth, God taketh away so I humbly enjoy my day.

I study music not knowing what I'm studying. It's about a feeling, it's in me, an eternal knowing.

You say I'm getting old and I guess that's true. But then I'll go to heaven--how about you?

It raises the soul, makes connections in the brain, takes us to a higher level vs. music of the devil.

Do it. If you postpone it you'll forget it and someone will come and they'll see it.

God gave us our ancestors and our genetic link to them and they are like best friends.

GOD RAISES ONE AND PUTS THE OTHER DOWN

Success is not from the east nor west but from God who puts one down and the other up--His best.

GENIUS IS HELD DOWN

From rags to riches and beauty from ashes--that's the natural progression when free of asses.

There's only one definition of a safe driver: when the riders can relax--note this fact.

Affluence has nothing to do with maturity, good character, vision, or especially wisdom.

They will always know you got most and that's a slow roast and now you've a right to boast.

THE SIN OF SLOTH

It's not a sin that'll send one to hell nor a crime that'll send him to prison but don't be sloppy son.

The Lord has vindicated me. After going through all that treachery He blessed and set me free.

There's no way power can be faked. He's a real man--or he isn't-- and it shows in his face.

Do it/buy it now. You gotta act as though it's gonna fold tonight and be prepared for a terrible blight.

Complete apathy is a measure of your fame later, as everything reverts to the opposite with haters.

When your brain waves go up, so to everyone in the room even if asleep--so stay high, don't stop.

Take time to go into the moment, and go deep. You're missing much by tracking mind, see?

Let freedom of mind be your goal. Disengage from all previous matrices making you old.

Nothing done, yet nothing left undone. Just see the goal then productively putter (have fun).

GENIUS IS HELD DOWN

DIVINE APPOINTMENT: DO YOUR THING

Now's the time to do your thing: the divine appointment before your birth to write, dance or sing.

Your genius is a mere potential–it must be developed by overcoming obstacles, substantial.

The family can be great or a human zoo. Fairies and Greek tragedies create mental illness too.

I'm in a new land, away from danger. I made friends though a stranger and God's not done yet, I wager.

Genius needs uncommitted time. Train the dogs, cats and kids you are not available until noon, your line.

Put silliness and clutter in the same bag. These are mental hazards irritating as a nag.

After 60 be grateful for every day. That's the best way to live then every day's a party: hurray.

More and more I want to be alone. I want to live in my head and happily create from my throne.

I can not find my destiny with out total solitude. Like a ton off my shoulders, free of the rude.

You're exceptional, hardworking, inventive and good. That's not true of the others with hearts of wood.

Less is more (more mircroscopic is more macroscopic) so get into the moment for thought galore.

Nothing's as good as staying home. Every time I plan to go out I resent it or want to be alone.

SUPERIOR PEOPLE HAVE FEWEST FRIENDS

GENIUS IS HELD DOWN

Maslow found that superior people have very few friends. It's not superior to be social, amen?

Nothing out there is as good as being alone in my home. So I just don't go out, never to roam.

The Toad: The reptilian brain, purely appetitive. Desirous, clinging and hungrily manipulative.

Home is where we're the King while surrounded by all our things. Why go out? It's sin-enabling.

Go out and you eat wrong food, spend money needlessly and waste all your time. Stay home, buy online.

REPENTANCE BRINGS BOLDNESS

Repentance makes one bold. An unheard of level of courage in public comes from making gold.

Sin creates slurs, stutters and shakes. No true self-confidence here only the boasting of fakes.

Use two speeds: action or total relaxation, attitude adjustment, dropping out, back to zero, fun.

Now that I'm "off" all day I'm getting so much more done. Way to success and insight: have fun.

It's not about listening to music but rather having it as the background ambience to evoke thought.

Think of your sins this way: You got dirty from the mud all around but now by God you're renowned.

Sure you make a stab at it, but are you thorough? That's the word of the day: finish, be a hero.

As I tell my dog, it's not all about playing ball. That's life--everyone has to get serious or they'll fall.

GENIUS IS HELD DOWN

BAD PAST ALL ERASED

Forget the bad past, it's all erased through Jesus. But first repent then angels say "it pleased us".

The desire to acquire is a terrible tendency. Details of acquisitiveness never end, see?

Essential part of being a survivalist: Deciding the quintessential and eliminating the rest.

The saints sense superfluity. It makes them sick as they see junk and messy disorder as a tragedy.

Up and down stairs doing housework all day. Thighs are as tight as drums, no gym needed, ok?

Learn to love assiduity, thoroughness, tenacity and routine. Puritanism's a reaction to chaos and fiends.

When I was dishing it out it all came easy but when HE was the one, he was miserly, mean and stingy.

Beauty from ashes--how to be blessed: Simply re-invent while God re-writes the whole mess.

God's not the author of confusion but a sound mind. Order is godly and disorder's of the devil--a sure sign.

The man at the top has a clean desk. Don't be a cluttered junkman, clarify to be your best.

Stop feeling remorse about what the demons did through you. They work through the weak or the flue.

IT WASN'T YOU BUT DEMONS COMING THROUGH

It wasn't you it was demons comin through you cuz you're weak but that's the past, so now: speak!

GENIUS IS HELD DOWN

I don't need to be defined by my work anymore. I know I'm defined by God as my spirit soars.

Please adopt a puppy or kitten and give it a good home! That's your therapy for any syndrome.

Use your mind now. You can get out of anything if you cut it loose then re-enter the flow.

All of life reflects the sin process: of purity, temptation, sin/loss and then the rewards of redemption.

In the Fallen Hero Syndrome, sin brings a spiraling down and then persecution is reflected all around.

If I'm nice to him he'll be nice to me. It's all the approach: if I'm a raving bitch he'll fight back/see me differently.

All I can do is take everything out and add it back one at a time to test response. Same with people, alas.

Genius, mystic or infantile seems the same. Problems when mind is tracked--don't play that game.

You want things neat and orderly, and you're a minimalist: just the most essential and nothing amiss.

TURNING POINTS

Let today be a turning point in your life. Beauty from ashes: in the twinkling of an eye, gone is all strife.

What you need is closure. You've been pining long enough--any longer will definitely ruin your future.

God has an appointed time for every matter He has planned--but impatience makes life so bland.

There are benefits to trouble. When God shows up you get the glory, double (it's in the bible).

GENIUS IS HELD DOWN

God blesses so big even foes agree it was Him in your life. What a miracle being God's wife.

Those who live godly will suffer persecution. But suffering precedes greatness: it's a substitution.

Never argue with stupid people, they'll bring you down to their level and for us geniuses that is the devil.

Even good people go through bad times. It's good to know so when it hits it's not due to our "crimes".

Rude, condescending, doesn't reply and he lied. That's the worst--not a trustee bonafide.

SEE THINGS PROPHETICALLY

To maintain sanity see things prophetically. The Lord said this would happen, like breaking away.

Liberals put ideology above biology (species-specific diets), forcing vegan on their pets.

Alone in the wilderness I bypassed culture so as it was sinking in it's swill I was coming into my Lord's will.

I was invaded by an opposing culture of Generation X-ers and it was hell learning about evils of open borders.

I'm the opposite to the selfie generation--I hate having my picture taken.

Horrible: As each side increasingly demonizes the other, compromise becomes impossible.

Satan blocks through put-downs. They belittle, mock and reject but with God you'll remain big in town.

Why are we married? Cuz we both wanna be taken care of, see?

Must disown back to keep your reality intact: self-esteem healed by truth or your world goes black.

GENIUS IS HELD DOWN

I suffer, I write. That's how it's always been but when loose ends come together I'm higher than a kite!

Clear your head to get more productive. That means people too (they can be so rambunctious).

I live in a nice little community--I never see anybody. Freedom is so sweet I start my weekend on Tuesday.

We die and leave the grind. Keep that in mind when you think of what you'll leave behind.

Great equalizer is the herafter but cherish your lives. When we die no more ties: sister brothers husbands nor wives.

THE SAINTS ARE WISE AND WITTY

The saints are mercurial: wise and witty. It's natural when you see through people whether girl or bitty.

Take "me" out of the equation. Now you see so far: wide angled (ego-less) vision is elation.

He smoked so many meds they said he'd never preach but then GOD gave him a new voice to beseech.

Any focused poet knows it: he's gotta stay quiet in the moment to be heroic and potent (noticed).

In families there are honor killings but to a lesser degree verbal beatings/treacherous dealings.

The time has come to give up on them. They didn't see you as a gem and were quick to condemn.

Be a well-oiled timeless beauty. This is your duty once you know the truth--and it's not vanity, really.

Being broken is the best place cuz now you're open to God whereas before you wanted to be mod.

GENIUS IS HELD DOWN

LOOKING BACK WE SEE DEMONS

Looking back we may see demons. This can bring remorse (of course) but then understanding deepens.

Stop filling your mind with inferior stuff. It's such a weird debasement, thinking you're so tough.

Turn all input off, now put your music on. Thus trigger your inner field as the outer world's forgone.

Stop all outer noise and replace with music. The consequences of not doing so can be so tragic!

If you're real careful the symptoms will abate. But if you push it it's another chemical injury, changing fate.

To one with chemical sensitivities, getting into a car is like a gas chamber. I'm staying, a homie in God's favor.

TALK IS CHEAP

I love the way you speak but talk is cheap, you need results--and those frankly are up a creek.

The youth corps are exploding geometrically. Many don't speak English so we're in deep trouble, really.

Sin or disease? Since sin gains tragic hold--a possession--it's also a disease so repent, please.

As bad as it gets, focus on eternity. This life isn't your home but a shabby porch to a mansion, see?

Why do I write like that? It's my destiny. Why do I talk like that? Because it's urgent, for brevity.

Aging is saging: As the body recedes the spirit grows--this is conscious aging, being in the know.

Now's the time to break those ties. Before now it was peace at any price but

GENIUS IS HELD DOWN

now all loyalty has died.

DON'T RESENT CONTROLLERS, TAKE CONTROL

Instead of resenting controllers, take control. For resentment puts you beneath them, makes you old.

The worse things get the more you know you've a job to do. So be happy despite all and change your view.

Via computer I transcend circumstances and parochial nuisances--ignore bad and get into preferences.

The worse things get the closer you are to destiny bursting open. You were born for this, so be hopeful.

With God it's a startling comeback. But that's a moral revolution which to sinners seems a drawback.

Forsake concern for "likes". The less "likes" the more you know you're telling the truth to dense types.

SO MANY OPPORTUNITIES NOW

There will be plenty of opportunities for you--just repent, focus on your wants and wait for the cue.

Stop the shame for when the devil was in ya'. Anything can happen when controlled by his minions.

Enontiodromia: the put-down sister becomes the queen and takes em all in, forgiving the fiends.

Things became right when I learned to back down. Just pray and watch everything perfect all around.

The worse things get the more you know your destiny has come. For you were born for this time, hon'.

Enontiodromia: When bottom becomes top and the top becomes bottom--life reversals seen from Adam.

GENIUS IS HELD DOWN

LIFE IS A PIE: DON'T WASTE TIME!

Life is a pie: the more you spend on this the less you spend on that--so figure that out then fly.

It's too much to keep up with so redirect your energy, go within and detach frenemies.

I focused inward to my own family and friends. That collapsed the outer, from a clunker to a Benz.

The scandals are flying furious and faster. To keep up with it all takes time away from your own disasters.

I'd rather focus on this than that! Just this decision alone turns my reality to happy white from sad black.

ELIMINATE TO EXPAND

The end: things are closing in. What to do: Focus inward, eliminate to expand, repent of sin.

For the first time now I'm thinking more of heaven. We're a breath away from so much joy, no leaven.

Life's a pie so don't do that today, you've got better things, ok? What's your goal? On that piece stay.

In times of stress, a connection will be made. Let that percolate--the answer to all problems as an aid.

I have learned from fools and sages that SIN decides if you're a success on stages or locked in cages.

It's all by design: every part's been planned while their decline is imminent cuz we were nice every minute.

Choose your life level: Ignore what's going on, it doesn't apply. You're in your own groove, so fly.

They act so wise, these fools. Overcome respect, their tools. See reality and

GENIUS IS HELD DOWN

judge rightly--God's rules.

Recall: Life is a Pie. If you want success, spend less time with anti-success forces. Focus: the mostess.

So much coming all at once. Yet it still misses the zombies--though we stand against, they're still a dunce.

There's an evil side of riches cuz though we BUY our soul still itches for something more delicious.

If you gotta repeat everything twice is it bad hearing or ignoring what you say as an underling?

If you gotta repeat everything twice but you see he responds to his friends is it disrespect or a vice?

RICHES CAN MAKE MISCHIEF

Austerity has great rewards but riches are a mischief, having too many choices to get twisted.

You achieve success by *releasing obstruction*--becoming more austere, not an image-magician.

I invited them to profit from the solitude but they bled me wrecking my privacy too.

My new life started the day I got a wall around my house with a locked gate.

Simplicity makes happy but when choices expand you can lose your mind categorically.

When you get money again, don't mess up--keep the same routines developed when a grub.

Inconvenient women were burned as witches all through history. Don't be weird just be a mystery.

Austerity has great rewards but living rich can lead you down a ditch or make a witch.

GENIUS IS HELD DOWN

Have nothing to do with the world as it degrades more each day. Use Medium Chill, just get along--ok?

All you gotta do is brush your teeth, look sharp then show up! You've done all the preparations, look up.

I helped you and you rose up against me anyway. In defiance you wanted to betray and check my dossier.

AVOID LOGORHEA AND MANY WORDS

People don't see the impact of words. We smear ourselves by talking too much and conjuring up worlds.

When due respect becomes dense disruption, we must make way for others less open to corruption.

If something's wrong it's gotta go--be debunked. Not keep parts of it after it's flunked.

Be strong and thorough when eradicating evil. Not just partial or being talked back into it.

We don't deserve it just for being born--we gotta do the work like grow up/stop being a jerk.

Feeling unappreciated, Stockholm Syndrome made her yearn for their approval more--what a chore!

Some things are poison. That is the darkness of sin vs. Jesus risen. It is bleakness and sorrow, no vision.

I've always strived for meaning. To me it meant instant healing--it always stopped the heart from bleeding.

It's not about choosing sides but thinking outa the box. See what's really going on (awareness rocks).

The worse things get the more we realize our destiny. If it weren't so tragic it'd actually be funny.

GENIUS IS HELD DOWN

It is possible that marriage takes us the rest of the way--struggling for years but this has saved the day.

Call them out for their pettiness and indifference. They have no heart--say that, for instance.

It's not what you get but what you don't spend then spend right and that takes study day and night.

THE FEELING OF GOING BEYOND

The feeling of going beyond a problem--one that's been there forever! This is such a break in the weather...

When nothing to do, when bored, when the world betrays--then the happy inner illuminates, today.

Few know the difference between right and wrong nor do they care, in a pitiful descent into moral despair.

Why do You further the heathen and not me? Why ignore the saints who love You as Your devotees?

It's not the amount you get it's what you do with it. For you can waste a fortune so study and get with it.

Accepting the loss is like tithing so ask God to apply it for "equal benefit" and thus attitude is the gist of it.

Computers evoked latent talents: I experienced an explosion into success where I had been totally missed.

Every generation has it's own special socially-approved of sins but it's all destined for the trash bin.

ANTICIPATE WHILE YOU WAIT

You work, you plant a seed. Now you relax and enjoy the moment while you wait--that's my creed.

Must clear the decks for the inner to illuminate. It's like removing a hex so

GENIUS IS HELD DOWN

don't worry loss of mate.

If they assemble against you they shall fall. Isiah 54: 15

Whatever they think, genius thinks the opposite. This is discovery as he shoots up like a rocket.

When they rise up against you, you know you're on track since the mass is false and only a few have the facts.

Don't petty fog everything with trivia. Insignificant details just blunt your force whether phone or media.

Don't conform to what they think as it changes in a blink and the truth's unchanging whether in word or ink.

They're always trying to get my attention and ask me questions only to befuddle me and fog my direction.

If one is immature, money ruins them for sure. They spend it on themselves but it doesn't build allure.

WITH GOD NO ONE'S STUCK

With God no one's stuck. No matter what, in a second HE changes it all though it seems like luck.

Today I'm on vacation from distraction and it's gonna be a divine conversation with music (elation).

Wait for creativity to gestate. Think hard before opening the gate or it ruins your fate so wait--it won't be late.

If it's a family it acts like it, if not it doesn't (it's rot). Let it go and open up to God's family (all you've got).

Lower habits degrade then great beauty fades. Repentance brings order then it all returns in spades.

Leave behind false ties--those your values despise. Then a vista opens up: so glorious after those lies.

GENIUS IS HELD DOWN

To limit influence, whistleblowers are shunned by family. It's damaging if you don't agree or an anomaly.

In your darkest moments, escape through music. Look to heaven: under His wings be impervious to the tragic.

More than sin bringing family rejection, it's thinking different politically that destroys these connections.

Give them a funeral for they are dead to you and God. You're alive--ready to thrive--so just enjoy your ipod.

If weak, in marriage her defects illuminate (changing her fate). You must be strong to get along (so wait).

A rising tide raises all ships. These are friends you'll bring up with your success--have a great trip (no slips)!

OVERCOME ENVY FOR SUCCESS

Just when you overcome envy at another's success, God cleans up your mess and brings out your best.

I was broken, filled with addiction. It took years to build back up: to be strong with real convictions.

Forgive those who hated you when broken. It's the natural process of sin but now you're well-spoken.

Stop collaborating with evil because it causes upheaval and it's just as bad as acting like the devil.

Here you're a Christian meant to rule and lead and end up instead scorned, mocked and weak-kneed?

It is the best trip you could ever believe: all day long working magic miracles that God did conceive.

How to be creative. Clear the decks, open the mind, sever all ties to the cruel and unkind.

GENIUS IS HELD DOWN

Grace applies righteousness to sinful man. grace is the truth that sets us free: Free to just BE.

SELF-GENTLENESS IS KEY

For joy: Because self-gentleness is key, it's all a big party to me and the best part--it's all for free.

Turn it all off. You know it's all horrible so now just go inside and avoid those who scoff then blast off.

Become instinctive--you don't have to talk. Get out of social hebephrenia and prepare for great shocks.

Be an actor. Act like the human at his highest peak, not an ass: Act nobly but maintain a little sass.

Take rejection as a sign you're a gold mine, built on years of overcoming they can't understand (no fan).

The True Self is a unique seed symbol: the treasure hard to obtain--when they stop pulling your chain.

DUNCES IN CONFEDERACY AGAINST

Sign of genius: all dunces are in confederacy against him. Are you squeezed out? It's a complement man.

Finding the True Self takes years of suffering to burn the dross. Via culture, we become least not most.

Life is two-pronged: relaxation and creative action. Don't deny the former or you'll have inexaction.

Repent and God releases talents. Of deviation from this rule there is no allowance: Are you a star or dunce?

Trust for a turnaround now that we know we're about to come to blows with friends who are really foes.

No matter what we can still have prosperity. God is above all so love Him then

GENIUS IS HELD DOWN

proceed merrily.

If motives are good you can be as conceited as you please. The point is repentance: don't be a sleaze.

Our wrongfulness evokes their hatefulness: With repentance there is instead loving fullness.

Women set-off competitive strivings. This can be so viscous and conniving your soul may need reviving.

Caught-up in sin we're a trash bin. It's a system where all parts sync so keep their distance.

When broken I was chokin'--filled with tears and fears--but when God opened I felt focused and chosen.

STAY WITH CONFIRMERS

My mother said: "Stay around people who confirm you--by whom you're spiritually fed--then look ahead."

"Vengeance is mine." When you let people off the hook, they're now on God's--He'll punish the crooks.

I had to learn to back down (to submit and cast my care with a smile not a frown) to be a big fish in town.

Sin turns us inside-out. It's a degenerative state (drought) combined with mental illness and self-doubt.

If you don't back down it's brinkmanship which escalates. This is making gold, transforming energy and your fate.

It was hard learning to submit to my husband. But once I did things went smoothly with much abundance.

Make your lines simple and easy to know over land and sea. The simpler the better--that's truth, you see.

Work while the sun shines, plant a seed. Then relax and wait for God to meet

GENIUS IS HELD DOWN

every one of your needs.

Block the gross, evil or macarbre things from coming to mind. Be a gentle child--stay sweet and kind.

It's all the influences you surround yourself with that determine the real you, so be careful or be blue.

To know that you're there, you need an echo. You're blessed finding your soul-mate (true beau).

Marriage is true freedom for the female. Don't listen to harridans advising divorce--they oughta be sent to jail.

"Because of who I am, I stick to my husband whether I like him or not, even if at times it may feel like rot."

As long as I'm sober, I trust my creative instinct: Whether understood or not, I just know what I ought.

DECIDE TO END YOUR REACTIONS

Decide to end your reactions to people. Now you create, they react--not they flub up and you're cracked.

At first they envied her but when it turned to hate she took it on and fell right down, pitifully dumbed down.

Existential envy is the basis of all human troubles. Life's a struggle as they cause one to stumble.

She loved them so when they hated her for her looks she fell right down--the smart lady became a clown.

After their envy caused rejection her success-in-reaction brought an even greater disaffection.

They were so bad themselves but that didn't matter--they hated her and would never forgive her, ever.

Severely limit TV to "not before 4 pm" or the like. See the danger and spend

GENIUS IS HELD DOWN

most of the day on hikes.

Despite all, I'm grateful things worked out the way they did: I'm still a kid, off the grid and of foes I'm rid.

Who are the foes? Those envying who you are (a star) and though you're nice they call you bizarre.

She was testy until beaten to adapt and that's when she matured in fact: not to love this crap but God, her Dad.

I go through things--who doesn't? Though it may seem strange, just being creative brings judgment.

PLATITUDES TO AVOID JUDGMENT

They learn to say nothing (platitudes) to avoid judgment. Ok--live that way while you become abundant.

They are completely empty. A dark cavern with a smiley on it--question their beliefs and they get testy.

A smiley cloaking emptiness--watch out. If involved you get hurt but don't pout: you chose the drought.

You know you're mature (true self) when you stop following people and just stand high as a steeple.

Come out of depression, it was a person infecting you. It's a contagious madness eclipsed by the untrue.

Feel crazy/anxious? This is where music comes in. It's soothes/excites but not that cheap globalism.

MR. AND MRS. SMILEY

Mr. and Mrs. Smiley (covering-emptiness) is everywhere. No heart, black art-- godless and insincere.

Since we're punished for loving God, few know the power therein. That's why most are weak or rely on spin.

GENIUS IS HELD DOWN

The devil really did make you do it . You were so empty he took you over cuz in morality you weren't fluent.

You can't "be nice" into heaven, or work your way. Just love Jesus each moment, every single day.

We all know genius can't fit but now it's expected to or not seen as legit and it's a mess--cool it.

There's three bases for depression: sin, food or anti-depressants (what you take to self-medicate).

Stop enabling! Just hold your head up high and be king: state the truth whether you write or sing.

You're the best in whom all now invest. You've worked all your life to get to here: an elder coming to his crest--with zest!

DON'T TRACK YOUR MIND

Don't track your mind like that! Forgive, forget the rat or your work gets pat as the creative goes flat.

The relationship must work through past introjects to become whole and happy or things turn crappy.

Genius sees between the lines: the "opposite is true" mentality, seeing way beyond the obvious (banality).

Anti-depressants started a train wreck of bizarre behavior lasting forty years and an ocean of tears.

The principals of lust don't change: it'll bring you down, derange and the years of waste you can't gage.

Self-confidence you can't fake--of these phonies I've had all I can take! Look beyond self, for God's sake.

Give up old templates. At first one feels empty but then there is great relief: you've caught the energy thief.

GENIUS IS HELD DOWN

The oldsters are soon dead and youth were never led. Stop hankering for the past and go to where you're fed.

If you don't geographically relocate in the next six months you'll be blocked from moving--good luck.

Stop right now and just enjoy this long weekend: our sure cure for election exhaustion.

As a Christian woman I must listen to my husband though I may find it a problem, amen.

Extreme sensitivity becomes extreme beauty once you get it altogether. If not, it's stormy weather.

I got all this cuz I'm kind to animals and God rewarded my heart. Persevere, keep at it and never stop!

Alcoholism: If your grandparents/great grandparents had it I wouldn't chance it cuz it's very genetic.

SWAMP UPDATES

Critical Race Theory [Race Essentialism] pits people against each other based on their color.

Putin's trying to help us cuz he doesn't wanna see America wicked, corrupt and feminized.

The fight for equality has turned into aggressive dogmatism bordering on absurdity. Putin

Proof the mandates are about oppression not safety: The migrants don't have to be vaxxed see.

Globalism is communism with an elite at the top and no middle class save enforcers & favorites.

When other hotel visitors complained about the Afghan public urination they were called "racist".

GENIUS IS HELD DOWN

Every black republican is a white supremacist. [Anonymous quote from a reverse racist].

Most women don't think for themselves. They listen to their neighbors, friends and CNN myths.

The Great Reset Plan thru covid: make us all destitute and wreck the economy totally, that's it.

"A black youth with a book is acting white"--by Barrack Obama the biggest racist in America, aye.

They've been preying on white guilt but for the first time ever pulling the race card didn't work.

The most shocking information: The socialists called the "squad" actually believe their positions.

"Under no circumstances should Biden concede, but Trump should immediately concede"

Dead people don't ordinarily vote but when they do they vote by mail. Rep. Matt Gaetz

In the swamp you don't have to mean what you say it's all about keeping family businesses going, ok?

Psalms 144: He trains our hands for war. He reveals their strategies and lays out our counterattack.

FAITH is the channel chosen for winning. If they can destroy our faith, we'll be forever losing.

Weaken and destroy our faith, use the evil power of unbelief against us: this is what we face.

NOT A NICKEL TO A LIBERAL

Jerry Lewis disinherited five sons. Remember that when the time comes--not a nickel to a liberal hon'

GENIUS IS HELD DOWN

The Lord shall cause your enemies who rise up against you to be defeated before you. Deut. 28: 7

Just realize you'll have these battles--to toughen/make you perfect--but don't fear them at all.

Your foe will come out against you one way and flee 7 ways and so you see? Don't fear treachery.

When I think of all the things that could've happened but didn't cuz God is always with us as promised.

We're fighting mighty powers in a dark unseen world not flesh and blood. Remember that to stay good.

Process: I was attracted to a negative element and a self-induced tragedy made me forever turn from it.

We are called to live by Christ's standards even if that requires a season of isolation, decades even.

I was attracted to certain things and one bad event trashed these appetites/tendencies quick.

PUT ON THE NEW SELF

We put off the old self, corrupted by its deceitful desires, and put on the new man with aristocratic attire.

The new self is created to be just like God, in true righteousness and holiness. Be that sis.

Joe Biden smiles when he lies and he smiles when he's caught lying, it's so second nature to him.

Biden will open up the borders and take all the guns. He's a Chinese agent, that's why he's so rich hon'.

If AOC runs the floor it will be the reason the democrats have the smallest majority since WWII.

GENIUS IS HELD DOWN

The reward for repentance is right-brain living: like continuous miracles in cornucopia.

You'll be famous suddenly cuz that's how it works. suddenly, after a long wait, you'll get the perks.

The Creative Act is an actual structure in nature. It has a beginning, an end then a reward for sure.

Creative Act is what it is--you can't artificially truncate it and say "this is the end", to my consternation.

Unremunerated work for decades then one fat check, that's the way it is with discoveries, that's a fact.

After the Creative Act return to play like a kid on Saturday.

The desert symbolizes spiritual happenings thru history and thus I constrain to it in movie/memory.

It just **LOOKS** like overnight success but actually took many decades of hard work and messes.

It's very simple to predict the future: on the track record of the past. To the clear that's obvious.

Do your work and don't present it til it's ready. Don't force the fit to achieve and come off silly.

DETOX OR DIE

There comes a moment where body decides to release all its toxins. Could be eczema, anything.

The death shots bring on blood clots, heart attacks, strokes, embolisms, lungs fill up drowning.